A Bobby's Job

A Bobby's Job

Some recollections of thirty years' policing

by

Bill Hannis

First published in Great Britain in 2003 by
Etone Publishing
40 Sheep Street
Shipston-on-Stour
CV36 4AE

Reprinted 2006

ISBN-10: 0-9544624-0-8
ISBN-13: 978-0-9544624-0-6

Produced by Action Publishing Technology Ltd, Gloucester

For

Dad's three girls

Doreen, Julia and Natalie

BOBBY'S JOB

An expression used in North Warwickshire to
describe a sinecure: a job requiring little or no
effort with much recognition and status

Contents

Chapter One

Joining the Job

How did I get to this? The middle of the night of 22 November 1974: I am standing with a loaded gun in my hand ready to kick open the door of a family house in a residential suburb of Birmingham, looking for IRA terrorists. I am the only armed man with a group of fourteen detectives seeking those responsible for killing and maiming many, many, people as a result of two bombs in pubs in Birmingham city centre. I always hoped when I dreamt of being a detective that I would investigate murder, but I thought that it would be of the Sherlock Holmes type, all deduction and brilliance, not searching of premises in pursuit of those responsible for mass murder and destruction.

The idea of being a policeman came in my mid teens. It was actively discouraged at home and school. Mother had always thought I should be a vicar or a doctor, and my brother build bridges, which he went on to do very successfully. We were a one-parent family; our father had not returned from the war. He had not been killed, he just did not come home.

The careers master at the local grammar school at Nuneaton did not see the Police Force, as it was then known, as a career. Mother and school pointed me at the Probation Service. A job placement was found at Hinckley

1

Probation Office on Saturdays. It was a very strange Saturday job: sitting in on interviews between a well-meaning Probation Officer and the local hooligans. I obtained a provisional place at Leicester University to read sociology and psychology. The proviso was two A levels but I only passed one, geography.

The failure did not deter school or mother. It was arranged that I would retake physics at Christmas along with the local vet's son. Leicester would hold a place for me for the following year, 1962.

I decided that I did not wish to return to school or become a Probation Officer. I waited until Mother was at work, dressed in my best, and went to Nuneaton police station where I asked to see the Superintendent. The office Constable asked my reason and I informed him that I wished to discuss joining the Warwickshire Constabulary. The enquiry hatch slammed shut and a short while later a smiling Sergeant invited me through an adjacent door into an office.

I told the Sergeant that I wanted to join the police. I believed that a recruit could join three months before their nineteenth birthday and attend the Police District Training Centre, being sworn in as a Constable at nineteen years during initial training. The Sergeant told me that this had recently changed and that the minimum age for acceptance was nineteen years. I was eighteen years and five months. The Sergeant decided to see whether I fitted the minimum requirements. Height, weight and chest expansion were absolute requirements and there was no exception to the minimum levels. I was pronounced suitable and then discovered that my one A level and ten O levels, insufficient for Leicester University, exempted me from the police entrance examination.

I was quickly subjected to two short interviews, one with an Inspector and another with the Superintendent. Following the interviews, Sergeant Burn, the recruiting Sergeant, asked whether I would join as a Cadet until my

2

19th birthday. I readily accepted and filled in the appropriate form. There followed in the next few weeks interviews at police headquarters at Leek Wootton and a medical at Warwick.

The medical was undertaken by Doctor Worthington, a Police Surgeon. He had a surgery in his wonderful mock-17th-century house in Jury Street, Warwick, adjacent to the East Gate. It was disconcerting to stand naked in the front room of a house abutting the street with double-decker buses passing the house. The colour blindness test was to distinguish two colours of some very old and dirty skeins of wool which he kept in his desk drawer – difficult under any circumstances.

I satisfied all criteria and was offered a post as a Police Cadet, commencing in 1961 at £6 per week. I was to work in plain clothes as it was considered wasteful to supply a uniform for five months.

Such excitement – a plain-clothes policeman at eighteen and a half! Mother was disgusted; she considered all policemen to be rogues and drunkards, an opinion no doubt reinforced by her daily observation of the Nuneaton Police Club, the entrance to which was visible from the sitting room of our house. I was soon to find out for myself if her opinion was justified.

I was a unique item at Nuneaton police station, eighteen years seven months and no uniform. The training Sergeant, the same Sergeant Burn who also dealt with recruiting, was unable to fit me into the training programme with the other final stage cadets. These were undertaking beat patrol and motor patrol attachments. A simple training programme was devised for me: a spell in the front office; a fortnight in the traffic office; attendance with other cadets on training days at Headquarters and the remaining time attached to CID.

Indoctrination in the front office consisted of switchboard and tele-printer training and a baptism of fire at the enquiry hatch dealing with the enormous range of problems brought

3

to the police station. My first encounter with Mrs Bates on her regular Friday visit was a nightmare. She lived next door to men from Mars and came every week to report their activities to the Superintendent. On this first meeting she had brought with her a pint bottle of milk, unopened, which she wanted analysing as the Martians had poisoned it. I told her to wait whilst I sought advice. The two office Constables were convulsed with laughter – they had been listening to every word. I was advised to take the milk, which I did. The Constables used it in their tea, but Mrs Bates came back later and asked for her milk. The bottle was hastily topped up with water and returned as non-toxic.

The most valuable lesson I learned in the front office was from PC Bob Murphy. Bob said that I should always address men as Sir and women as Madam, until I knew who they were, and not speak unless giving or seeking information. He was obviously an old soldier and in fact a Colonial Policeman also. He did not, of course, adhere to his own advice.

The whole five months was a delight, the time in the CID especially so. I was engaged in menial office duties, filing, tea making and running errands for much of the time, but I was also allowed to accompany detectives to the scenes of burglaries and on several occasions sit in on interviews with criminals being dealt with by DC Brian. I was amazed by the interview techniques which persuaded determined criminals to confess, when there was little or even no evidence. There was no violence or intimidation – it was basic 'trade puffing' with the use of one of many stock stories. I later used these methods to great effect over a number of years.

It was during these five months that I discovered the internal rivalries, the propensity for rumour and gossip and the outright jealousies of certain factions. Two incidents highlight this internal strife.

The Superintendent, Alec W Spooner, was known as Mr Wue, as his car was a Ford Zephyr with the registration WUE 999. As a well-known Warwickshire senior Detective, now in uniform, he kept a tight eye on the CID, which was resented. Two officers decided that Mr Wue was fiddling his car allowance and took daily odometer readings from his car and compared these with his log book which they purloined from the administration office. They were caught and suffered immediate transfer. Neither suffered in the long term, both progressing in the service.

The funniest incident was when one PC Eric, a somewhat rebellious car driver, was given a new partner. Eric's first task was to acquaint the new man with all the idiosyncrasies, shortcomings, rumours and gossip about the personnel at Nuneaton, in particular the senior officers. The briefing took place in the patrol car, parked in a lay-by on the A5 Watling Street. Eric was unaware that the handset of the radio was resting on the parcel shelf and in transmission mode. The whole of his diatribe was being broadcast to the head-quarters' control room. Eric's voice was recognised and Nuneaton informed. The Superintendent asked for the trans-mission on 'talk through' so that he could hear it, forgetting that every radio in Warwickshire could also hear it. Eric's traffic colleagues immediately set up a search and after some thirty minutes, a total of nearly an hour, he was found.

Eric was grounded and put on office duty for a period where he exasperated the Superintendent further by pretend-ing not to recognise his voice when he rang in to ask for a situation report one evening. I was amazed to see the same officer sitting one day with an unconnected telephone, picking it up and saying 'Nuneaton police station, can I help you?' for half an hour at a time under the supervision of a Sergeant. No doubt the police equivalent of doing lines at school.

Eric remained at Nuneaton for the rest of his service and on retirement became the Civilian Coroner's Officer. He was a very caring, considerate and efficient officer to the public, a loyal friend and an absolute nuisance to everybody else. The officer he was briefing in the car ended his career as a Chief Superintendent in West Yorkshire.

Cadetship was a wonderful insight into the police and also fostered a determination to be a detective.

5

March 1962 soon arrived, with measurement and fitting for uniform, final medical and allocation of collar number. Warwickshire always re-used collar numbers of retiring or resigning officers before allocating a new number. I was allocated 202, the collar number of DC Norman Clack, another pointer to CID!

Training was a total of sixteen weeks: two weeks' induction training, thirteen weeks at the District Training Centre and then a local procedure course. The induction course was at Leek Wootton Headquarters. The journey was by personnel carrier from Nuneaton. The regulations were such at the time that it was compulsory to travel to duty in uniform. The feelings of an eighteen-year-old dressing in full uniform including helmet, truncheon and whistle to walk the half mile from home to police station can only be imagined. I was in fear of being stopped and asked to deal with some situation, for unlike the Metropolitan Police we did not wear an armband to indicate whether on or off duty.

The induction course included drill instruction, then an important part of training. It was no problem for the ex-Forces recruits or myself as a former ATC cadet, but a nightmare for some and one in particular who could not swing his arms in opposition to his legs – a very comical sight, but a burden to the officer. There were twelve recruits, four cadets, some ex-service men, and one lady, who went through the whole of her training without a uniform (she was an odd shape but not beyond the capability of a decent tailor). An ex-RAF policeman arrived on the first day in full police uniform and shining brown boots.

Initial training of thirteen weeks took place at Number Four District Police Training Centre Ryton-on-Dunsmore. Most of the training was by rote and the discipline strong. The training consisted of instruction in law, practice and procedure, drill, self-defence, PT, swimming, civil defence and traffic duty.

All the instructors were police officers seconded from local forces, and their abilities were varied. There were a number of written examinations and the easiest way to prepare was to learn whole sections of the instruction manual by heart. I found no real difficulty with any aspect of the training other than swimming. As a non-swimmer, I had to be able to swim a width of Rugby swimming baths, unaided, by the end of the course. This was achieved by my being taught to float on my back and propel myself across the pool by flapping my hands and kicking my feet. Fine in a still pool, but a recipe for drowning in any other water.

Traffic duty was practised to the strains of the Blue Danube waltz, the hand signals keeping time with the music. Once mastered, they were put into practice by directing other recruits pretending to be cars, and then the final test: directing the instructors in their cars.

The thirteen weeks produced lasting friendships and despite the strict sex segregation, a number of relationships, some leading to marriage. There were also some disasters. One Birmingham City officer fell in love with a girl from Southend-on-Sea. With her encouragement he applied and was accepted into the Southend-on-Sea Borough Police. Sadly, by the time he had transferred she had fallen in love with someone else. He returned crestfallen to Birmingham.

The passing-out parade was usually the highlight of the course, but we on course 353 were to be honoured by the presence of R A Butler, the Home Secretary. This honour meant that no-one was allowed to have any guests at the parade. The painting and polishing would have done credit to a guards' brigade depot, and there was even a continuity drill squad of which I was a very proud member.

The excitement of passing out was only surpassed by the excitement generated by waiting for our postings. I knew that I would not be sent to the Nuneaton division of Nuneaton, Bedworth and Atherstone as the ruling on postings to home towns was very strict. The day arrived when the Warwickshire list was posted on the notice board at Ryton. 'PC 202 W D Hannis – Rugby.'

Chapter Two

On the Beat

Rugby. I had never been there. Although it was only sixteen miles from Nuneaton, my knowledge was limited to two sources – geography lessons and Thomas Hughes. The former told me that Rugby was a major railway junction and the home of heavy electrical industry, and the latter was Tom Brown's view of Rugby which was hardly relevant to modern policing.

The twelve original recruits to Warwickshire all survived the course although there was a considerable drop-out rate over the following years. Six out of twelve completed thirty years' service. We all returned to Leek Wootton for local procedure instruction and then the great day arrived when the divisional personnel carriers arrived to take us to our police stations. There were three of us for Rugby, and on arrival we were welcomed by a jolly and friendly Sergeant Palmer, a former naval officer. We were allocated shifts and told to report the following morning for familiarisation, but first we had to be taken to our lodgings.

I was billeted with an elderly widow, not far from the station. An end of terrace house, no bathroom, no central heating, no inside toilet, home from home. She was friendly and welcoming and asked if I liked tomato soup, which I did. This was fortunate for I was given it every day for three and a half years. My landlady suffered from selective deafness – she was deaf if she did not want to hear what you were saying. This deafness occurred whenever I suggested a change of menu or additional comforts. Wages were about £10 per week and the lodgings were £6. There was little or no chance of finding new lodgings, as there were, at that time, many apprentices in Rugby whose hours and money were better than ours, so you had to make the best of it.

The first two weeks of your career was spent in the company of an older Constable. This was known as 'showing you round'. In this two weeks, you needed to learn the boundaries of all the beats, and the position of all telephone kiosks which were used as 'points'. We were required to 'make a point' every hour. This involved standing by a telephone kiosk five minutes before and five minutes after the appointed time on the hour, half, or quarter. The times were staggered so that someone was available for most of each hour somewhere in the town. The only radios were in the police vehicles. The points also enabled the Sergeants and Inspectors to visit officers without searching the whole of the beat. It was also necessary to learn the location of all vulnerable property which had to be checked twice during each night shift. An undiscovered burglary on your beat resulted in arousal from bed followed by searching questions. How times change!

The officer 'showing you round' was also responsible for training you in reporting people for offences, generally minor traffic matters. The patience of the public in accepting not only being reported for a 'no waiting' offence, but also by a nineteen-year-old under supervision, was quite remarkable.

The first two weeks also included indoctrination into traffic point duty. Rugby was one of the few towns in Warwickshire with a permanent daytime traffic point in the town centre. It was with considerable fear and trepidation that I went for my first live practice. The comparison between the Blue Danube and standing in the middle of a four-road junction for a full hour directing heavy traffic was extreme. Some ten minutes after starting the Inspector and Sergeant arrived to assess me. I was allowed to continue and must have been satisfactory. The point was manned from 8am to 6pm, one hour on and one off. The duty was known as point and one beat, or one beat and point, thus indicating first or second hour. A shift was eight hours with forty-five minutes' refreshments. On a cold, wet, winter day it was an arduous task.

The public also used the point man as an enquiry office and came into the middle of the road to ask directions and advice. The local bus drivers also played a game to see how close they could pass without hitting you. There was no box or platform to stand on.

Shifts were 6am to 2pm, 2pm to 10pm and 10pm to 6am. Each 'turn' lasted two weeks, with days off in rotation. The probationary period for Constables was two years, during which time you could be dismissed at any time as 'unlikely to make a satisfactory officer'. No other reason was necessary and some supervising officers held it like the sword of Damocles. Discipline was strict: 'idling and gossiping' was a disciplinary offence, as was leaving your designated beat without good reason.

The great day arrived when I was allowed out on my own. I was on 6am to 2pm. It rained all morning. I was determined to report someone for something on my first day. I could then write the details in the station occurrence book, a huge ledger with wooden covers in which every occurrence on the shift had to be recorded. There was nothing, no expired tax discs, no parking offences – not even a pedal cyclist failing to conform to a halt sign. I was beginning to despair when at 1.45pm on my way into the station from my outside beat, I saw a car with engine running parked and unattended. I knocked on doors until I found the driver. He was incensed when I told him that I was reporting him for 'quitting'. I had discretion, of course, but failed to exercise this in my keenness. My supervisors failed to exercise their discretion either. The poor man was fined £7.10s (£7.50).

So began a thirty-year career – hardly the excitement of novels or films but a wonderfully satisfying day for me.

The two-year probationary period was a continual training programme with divisional training days, instruction in first aid and driving, residential continuation courses, and attachments to administration, traffic and CID. The intervals were continual shift work on the beat.

I was very keen but soon found that this keenness was not reflected in all my colleagues or supervisors. On one occasion I found five boys ranging in age from twelve to fifteen 'scrumping'. I got them all together intending to give them a warning and then found that they were carrying various stolen items: cycle capes, bicycle pumps, an umbrella and a torch. I questioned them and they readily told me where they had stolen them. I arrested them all and walked them over a mile to the police station. The station Sergeant was not amused and clearly did not want the trouble of dealing with five juveniles. He warned them all and released them without informing their parents. He did, however, compliment me on my diligence. I am a great believer in giving 'every dog a bite', but all five became regular customers during the following years.

Traffic and other minor offences were now routine, but I was yet to make an arrest for a crime. My chance came when I was designated for evening observation duty in the car park of the local cinema. There had been a spate of thefts from cars and motorcycles and also thefts of pedal cycles.

I concealed myself under a tree in the grounds of the Crown Cement offices and awaited developments. An hour had elapsed when I saw a man examining the row of motorcycles. I was very excited, but apprehensive: remember that we had no radio. I was on my own. It was dark apart from the illumination in the car park and street. I watched the man as he bent down and appeared to be unscrewing something, but then someone else came into the car park. My man was up and away, but only walking. I moved and

11

intercepted him, identified myself and searched him. No stolen property! I had jumped too soon. He did have a screwdriver and I walked with him along the row of motor cycles. I was not sure which machine he had been tampering with but I examined the rear of one and lo and behold, the rear light cover came off in my hand. I arrested my man, whose name and date of birth I can still recite, and cautioned him. He denied doing anything wrong. I walked my first proper prisoner to the police station (about half a mile), remembering not to release my hold on him whatever he said. I was rather worried what the station Sergeant would say about my attempted theft but found that he was pleased that someone had been caught. The cinema manager had been complaining!

A prisoner for crime required CID assistance and accordingly DC Peter came to help. I soon found that 'help' meant 'take over'. DC Peter interviewed the prisoner, wrote all statements, prepared the file and I signed everything. The case eventually came to court and I was required to give evidence in a 'not guilty' for the first time. A conviction and fine ensued: I was thrilled. I had a big write-up in the *Rugby Advertiser*. I thought I was ready for Scotland Yard.

Rugby was not a busy station compared with others, but there was a wide variety of incidents and because you worked alone, without immediate assistance, you learned self-reliance and developed confidence. Your tongue became your greatest weapon of self-defence. The advice when called to a fight was to pick the big one – it worked on most occasions. There were domestics to deal with, though a nineteen-year-old, an unmarried officer, advising a long-married couple on their problems was somewhat daunting.

Attachments to traffic and CID were dual purpose – experience for the probationer and an opportunity for the department to look at potential recruits. It was the luck of the draw as to whether anything occurred which enabled you to impress during a two-week attachment. It was essential therefore to impress during everyday work. It meant in my case to impress the Detective Inspector by solving a big case!

The chance came one Saturday evening. I had finished at 10pm and returned to my lodgings to shed my helmet and tunic and slip on a civilian jacket before walking to see my girlfriend who was staying at the home of a colleague. At about 10.15pm I was passing the cattle market near to the police station when I heard a female screaming. It was very dark in the market and I could not see anyone. I ran towards the sound which was clearly someone in extreme distress. I shouted and saw two male figures run out of the shadows into Railway Terrace and make off towards the railway station. I found a girl of about eighteen years lying on the ground; she was dishevelled and distressed. She told me that the men had dragged her off the street and were assaulting her. She said they were trying to rape her. I told her to go to the police station and tell the officer what had happened and that I was going to chase the men. All this happened in seconds. I set off in pursuit. I was young and fit and soon had them in view. I called on them to stop, which caused one to pause, enabling me to catch him. I did not waste time being too polite and called out to the other man who had stopped and was watching me with his friend.

I said, 'I know who you are, your mate has told me, you might as well give up.'

He did. I marched them back to the police station, in through the front door and there stood the girl with the Duty Inspector.

The girl said, 'That's them.'

I took the men to the charge office and began to document them. I was quietly elated – I had prevented a serious offence and arrested the offenders. I could see a commendation looming.

It was not to be. An hour or so later, the Duty Inspector sent for me, congratulated me on my courage and diligence and then told me the girl did not wish to take proceedings. I

13

was furious and demanded to see her. This was refused. I left the station in a huff and went to visit my girlfriend. I was late for the first time, not to be the last, as she found when we married.

I was told the next day by the Office Constable that the Inspector had talked the girl out of making a complaint. He did not want people to think that there were attempted rapes in Rugby. The poor girl no doubt thought that she was to blame.

I had been taught to drive early in my probationary period. The instructor was a local traffic officer and the examiner from force headquarters. There was little chance to use the new skill as there were few cars and in any event, beat duty was a walking role. Mobile patrol for beat officers was by pedal cycle on the larger beats on the edge of town or by 'Noddy' bike. This was a water-cooled Velocette motorcycle. I was selected for tuition on the motorcycle.

Instruction was by a Rugby traffic motorcyclist, Mick Hill. He arrived at the local ambulance station where I was attending first aid lectures. Mick was on his patrol motorcycle and his previous pupil had ridden a 'Noddy' bike to the ambulance station. I was handed a reinforced helmet, which was a police helmet with cork lining. I was shown the controls and instructed, 'Follow me,' and off we went. There was no verbal communication during the lesson. I followed Mick Hill all over town for over an hour. I was feeling very pleased with myself as we approached the police station in Railway Terrace. I turned in to negotiate the archway leading to the yard and realised I had not turned enough and was going to hit the wall, I yanked the handle bars over to avoid the wall but the bike had a very restricted turning circle due to the radiator and the leg shields. The bike fell over, damaging the leg shields and panniers. I cursed and picked the bike up – it was still in gear! Off it went through the archway dragging me behind it. I had no control and was in some danger, so I let it go.

The bike careered on and smashed into a line of pedal cycles standing in a rack under the archway. The noise attracted attention and the Chief Inspector, Ted Higgs, came running into the archway and said, 'What have you done to the bike?'

I was lying on my front and felt somewhat aggrieved that no one enquired as to my condition. There was an immediate instruction that novice motorcyclists would in future be instructed in the basic skills on the market area opposite the police station before being allowed on to the road. I was called for instruction as soon as the Velocette had been repaired. Mick Hill took me on to the market area, but within five minutes I had collided with one of the stalls. I was immediately removed from the list of potential motorcyclists and have never ridden one since.

There were many incidents in the course of two years. One illustrates the changes in times and the other of my continuing belief in fate: 'meant to be' as I have often been told.

The first incident occurred when the shift was somewhat depleted and only two of us were available for beat patrol on six beats. The other officer was Bill Corder, a former Fleet Air Arm Matelot. I had first met him when I was a cadet at Nuneaton and he serving at HMS *Gamecock*, a dry posting at Bramcote outside Nuneaton. Bill was nearing the end of his service and having married a Nuneaton girl was looking to join the local police. Following initial training Bill was posted to Rugby where I was already serving. It was at his home my then girlfriend was staying on the night of the attempted rape.

Bill was allocated 1 beat, the town centre, and I, 2 to 6 beats. This posting entailed a great deal of walking to cover all the property during the eight hours. I was making my second point at the Central Railway station when I was informed by telephone that Bill had been assaulted and sustained a broken leg. He was detained in hospital. I offered to call on his wife, who lived nearby, but was told

15

that this was in hand. I was ordered to walk into town and cover 1 beat for the rest of the night. Two things resulted from the assault. Bill became a hero, although there is no doubt that his aggressive attitude provoked the assailants, and I became a gardener. Bill like all married probationers found it difficult to make ends meet on the poor wages and he had an allotment. The timing of the assault was at planting time. I volunteered to take on the task during his enforced inactivity. I received regular instructions from Bill and help from his wife Colleen. I have to say that the task did not encourage a love of gardening in me. Thankfully my future wife had green fingers.

The second incident decided my future. Towards the end of my two-year probationary period I had begun to pick up the bad habits of others in relation to paperwork. Cutting corners was the game. The investigation of some crimes was a thankless task which is why we beat officers were allowed to keep the crime reports. Cycle stealing was one such crime. There were many thefts of pedal cycles in Rugby. It was a time when the cycle was the favoured form of transport. The crime recording system was simple. Record the crime, complete a cycle description form for the criminal records office and search for the cycle in the usual places. The powers that be considered that one way to clear the crime was to encourage the complainant to look for the cycle themselves. This often resulted in a success, but sometimes the complainant failed to inform the police, thus leaving the crime as undetected which was bad for statistics.

It was common practice to fill in the box 'complainant revisited on . . .' with a fictitious date. The Detective Inspector and Superintendent had a 'thing' about this but could not catch anyone out without a lot of legwork, as few people losing pedal cycles had telephones. Sadly, or perhaps gladly, I fell foul.

The first I knew of my discovery was waking up at 1pm on a Sunday following a Saturday night shift with Sergeant Reg Poultney standing by my bed. This officer was a rigid disciplinarian not given to levity. He threw a set of car keys and a vehicle log book on my bed and instructed me to be at Sutton Coldfield police station at 3.30pm to see Superintendent Jones. I asked why and was told that a serious complaint had been made against me. I asked what the complaint was but was told, 'You will know when you get there.'

I dressed in uniform and walked to the police station to collect the car. I needed to ask for directions and then drove to Sutton Coldfield in a very nervous state. I was kept waiting for half an hour and then ushered into the Superintendent's office. Mr Jones was a large, bluff but kindly man who did not help my nerves by saying, 'Well, young man, you are in some serious trouble.'

I almost screamed, 'What is it?'

Mr Jones said, 'You have failed to see the complainant in a case of cycle stealing.'

I was so relieved, I said, 'Is that all?'

The Superintendent said, 'All! You are on probation, you will get the sack.'

I was mortified. I quickly admitted everything and was on my way within an hour.

The next morning, I was summoned before the Superintendent having completed another shift of nights. Mr Croker was quite apologetic and said that I was unlucky because the complainant in my case was a friend of the Detective Inspector who had casually asked whether the policeman had been in touch. A negative reply led to my capture. I asked for an indication of my fate and I was told that I would appear before the new Chief Constable Richard Matthews on a disciplinary charge.

I worked in something of a state until the day of the hearing arrived. It was a requirement that the defendant's Superintendent attended the hearing to give evidence of character before penalty was imposed. Terrifying!

Mr Croker said that I would travel with him in his own car to Headquarters. It was not a pleasant journey and little was said.

I had never seen the new Chief and I was to be his first disciplinary case. Two charges of 'making a false statement on an official report' were read. I pleaded guilty. The facts were presented and the Chief asked if I had anything to say. I apologised and assured him it would not occur again (the classic response).

The Chief Constable started to talk about perjury and dishonesty and then said, 'Superintendent, is there anything you can say about this officer before I make a decision?' I felt doomed.

Mr Croker then gave a report on what sounded like the best recruit Warwickshire Constabulary had taken for many years. He produced a bundle of letters and said, 'These are from members of the public complimenting this officer on his conduct.'

I was amazed. I was only aware of one letter from an old lady who had got lost in the town centre. Mr Croker went on to say that he was sure that this was an aberration that would not be repeated. The Chief looked at me and told me that I was fortunate to have such support. How right he was. I was fined two days' pay.

The return was much happier. Mr Croker said that I was unlucky but someone had to be made an example of. He realised, he said, that it was unfair, and to make up for it, he and the Detective Inspector had decided that I would transfer to the CID after the dust had settled. I was to be in charge of stolen pedal cycle enquiries!

True to his word, in August 1964 at twenty-one years and five months, I was a detective.

Chapter Three

Rugby CID

The first day as a Detective was totally unexpected. I had anticipated being tasked not only with pedal cycles, but also with the filing of *Police Gazettes*, Crime Informations, and other publications from Criminal Record Offices throughout the United Kingdom. I was surprised to be told by the Detective Inspector to go home and return at 11pm. He explained that I would be required to join an observation team that was being established to catch a team of prolific burglars who had been targeting clubs and stealing the gaming machines, known at the time as 'one-arm bandits'.

I was then briefed further by the Detective Sergeant, Danny Wright. It transpired that during the previous week a farmer from Cathiron near Church Lawford had discovered a considerable number of sixpenny pieces and broken glass at some isolated farm buildings. The Detective Inspector had, on this Monday morning, called at the farm on his way in to work as there had been an overnight club burglary on the division. The Detective Inspector had found sixpences and glass. He was convinced that the burglars were using the site on a regular basis to break open the gaming machines after each burglary.

The plan was that each night from 11.30pm to 5.30am a team of four officers would lie in wait for the burglars to arrive and catch them red-handed. The buildings were some half mile from the road and a large iron rod was procured to

19

slip into mountings on the gate to prevent the exit of the villains' vehicle once inside the complex of buildings. The CID car was to be driven from its hiding place to block a second gateway. There were no personal radios, only a VHF set in the CID car. Staffing was such that the office was split into two shifts, 9am to 1pm and 11pm to 6am followed by a 2pm to 11pm, which resulted in each shift working an alternate night. It was expected that the operation would only take a week as the burglaries were very regular. It was not to be.

Two weeks later enthusiasm had waned, tiredness had set in and slackness followed. The original disposition of one man outside near the gate, one man in the car and two within the farm buildings relaxed to all four in a hay shed which had been turned into a very comfortable billet. In addition to the necessary food, beer was added which resulted in increased laxity.

They came. At 2.30 in the morning in a Jaguar saloon with three of us asleep and the fourth, who was having a walk, unable to warn the three in the shed as he was on the wrong side of the track. We awoke, and a whispered and frantic conversation resulted in a plan. I was to go to the car and hearing the blast of a police whistle, start up and block the drive. There was no time for the iron rod to be put in its mountings. The other two would sneak up on the burglars and blow the whistle when they were actually touching them. Sadly, our fourth member did not know of the plan and he jumped too soon. The whistle blew, the car failed to start, I heard shouting and then saw the Jaguar speed off up the track. My car started and as I set off, a figure ran in front of the car, not a colleague, so I drove at him. He leapt a hedge and I buried the front of the car in the hedge. Chaos, shouting, torches flashing, whistles blowing, but no arrests. Dismayed and very concerned as to the consequences, we quickly conferred on the best approach. A few lies were concocted for the Detective Sergeant who was patrolling in the vicinity and we contacted him on the radio.

Danny Wright was furious and disbelieving of our story.

No-one had seen the men clearly. There were at least three, probably four, one of whom had fair hair. Intelligence had suggested that two local Rugby men were involved. It was decided to watch their houses. I went to one house with another officer. We sat in an alley at the back of his house becoming more and more despondent until at about 6am we heard footsteps and some very heavy breathing. It was the suspect. We challenged him and after a brief denial he admitted that he had run all the way from Cathiron, some six miles, in the dark.

At the police station he would not implicate anyone but it was clear that the other main offender had to be his associate. He was arrested and interviews began. The result was that both admitted a large number of burglaries, implicating others in some of the offences. They also showed us where they had dumped all the gaming machines in the canal near to Cathiron.

We recovered some of the machines with the aid of grappling hooks, and others by the skill of our life-saving expert, PC 1 K D F Longcroft, who dived into the canal in his swimming trunks and recovered many machines and machine parts. Keith was at this time a traffic officer with CID ambitions. His readiness to carry out this hazardous task won him friends and soon a successful CID attachment followed.

I, as the newcomer to the department, was given the daunting task of preparing the file, but thankfully the assistance of Danny Wright resulted in him doing most of the work.

Some two years later, the same farmer rang the CID office to report that he had found one of his barns stacked with beer, spirits, crisps and chocolate. This was the proceeds of a burglary at Brandon Speedway Stadium the previous night. It was clear that the property was not abandoned and that observations would be required. The plan of two years previously was dusted off and at 10.30pm that evening I and three other officers, one in uniform this time, arrived at the farm.

As an old hand, I was in charge, and previous experience came in to play. We took fish and chips and plenty of beer. We had only just begun to arrange the hay into a decent seating arrangement, when they came! It was *déjà vu*. We were all in one place and could not get out without being seen. We soon realised that we were heavily outnumbered. There were twelve of them in three cars. The only radio was in the car which was hidden nearby so we decided to let them get into the barn, where they were probably going to have a party and then rush them, flashing torches, shouting, blowing whistles and 'tapping' people with our truncheons. There was a count of three and in we went. It was mayhem for a few minutes, but we soon had them all lined up with their hands on their heads, which is how they remained until the arrival of assistance in the huge shape of Sergeant Mick Fairfield, known as 'Fairy', and PC Charlie Patrick from Wolston. By the time the van arrived to take them all to Rugby, we had established everyone's part in the enterprise. All were charged, some with burglary and others with receiving stolen goods. The magistrates commended the four of us for our bravery in arresting 'these twelve young hooligans', this despite finding only four of the men guilty. The bench was very supportive in those days.

I was a detective at Rugby for two and a half years. The range of work was considerable. Theft, burglary, assaults, wounding, and a surprising amount of indecency including rape and buggery, but especially incest. There were cases of great amusement and others of enormous tragedy, though through it all ran the adage 'if you can't take a joke you shouldn't join'. This resulted in seeing the funny side of nearly everything and practical jokes abounded. Two which affected me related to my marriage to my lovely Doreen. The date of our marriage was set for December 1965 and as was normal, I had been allocated a police house: a little terraced house only six doors from the police station. The rear entrance opened onto the over-spill car park, kennels for

22

stray dogs and the police club. It was like 'living over the shop' and Doreen became the standby cook for prisoners' meals at weekends when the canteen was closed. The prisoners were never so well fed. We made no profit!

I had worked in my school days at a Bedworth Department Store selling furniture. I had long decided that when I was married I would buy two Leylux Wing chairs. I ordered these from my friend the furniture buyer, Frank Widdows. I also ordered basic furniture from him. These were the days when you furnished two rooms at the start of your married life. Frank gave me a continental headboard and a coffee table: some old stock. I, of course, told my colleagues of my good fortune and in due course the furniture was delivered to my house. This was before marriage and again, this being the 60s, we would not be living together until after the wedding.

Some days passed and I returned to the office after an enquiry one morning to find the office empty apart from a young cadet.

I asked, 'Anything doing?'

I was told, 'No, except for a message from Bedworth about some stolen furniture.'

I blanched and took the message from him. It was from DC Barry Butler from Bedworth and requested someone to ring him. I asked the cadet whether he had told anyone else of the message. He told me that he had not and I instructed him sternly to keep the matter to himself.

I asked the switchboard to put me through to Bedworth, another county station. I had great difficulty getting through, but eventually I managed to speak to Barry Butler. I casually enquired as to the circumstances of the case. Barry told me that he had locked up the manager from the furniture department at J C Smith's; the man's name was Widdows. Barry went on to say that the man had been stealing furniture for years and in order to try to extricate himself he had said that some of the furniture had been given to a policeman at Rugby. He would not give the officer's name but said that he was shortly to be married. Barry said that a coffee table had been mentioned as being among the stolen furniture.

As calmly as possible, I told Barry that I would follow up the enquiry and ring him back. I was told to hurry, as Barry needed to consider bail for the man Widdows.

My mind was racing, I could see the sack, disgrace, prison, disaster! I took the keys to the CID Hillman Husky Estate car and parked the car at the back of my house. I was carrying the headboard out through the back gate when all my CID colleagues appeared from the door of the police club, absolutely helpless with laughter. A complete con trick involving the switchboard operator and Barry Butler at Bedworth. The only innocent was the poor cadet.

The second joke was simpler, but very effective. Following my marriage my wife was working at Rugby Library and it was my pleasure, when shifts allowed, to walk up through the town and meet her from work. The walk was about three-quarters of a mile. It was autumn. I donned my raincoat and set off. I heard considerable laughter on my walk, but I did not connect it with me. I stood outside the library to wait for my wife. When she came out she said, 'What's that on your back?' There, for the whole town to see, was a pair of pink ladies' frilly knickers stapled to the back of my raincoat.

The CID at Rugby had no love for police dogs – we were often in jeopardy at scenes of crime from overenthusiastic dogs who seemed to see anyone not in uniform as a criminal. We had a particular 'war' with PC Peter Shingler and his dog Beta. We did not help the situation by banging on the side of Beta's van as we passed it in the yard. The constant barking became something of a blight on the life of PC Shingler. One sunny afternoon he caught one of us banging on the side of the van. The ground floor windows of the house, which were our offices, were open. Peter got the dog from the van and put her through the window. We scattered, some to a cupboard under the stairs, some to another office, which they locked, and two to the bathroom which was also the darkroom. There was much giggling, mainly with relief, and much barking from the dog.

Then we heard, 'Shingler, get this bloody dog out of here.'

We crept out to find the Detective Sergeant, Danny Wright, and a witness he had been interviewing standing on the desk in the Sergeant's office with Beta barking up at them. Needless to say, the teasing stopped.

A quiet Saturday afternoon brought real tragedy. My great friend Dick Leach and I were in the CID office having a quiet chat, following a pleasant Saturday lunch-time 'cultivating informants': a euphemism for having a few pints round the town. We were familiar with a family from a council estate from Bilton on the outskirts of the town. They were in a poor state, lots of kids, low income and parents of low intelligence. The boys were regularly in trouble for theft and other minor crime. We were aware that there was a young baby in the house and the gossip was that the mother was the eldest daughter of the family.

The daughter concerned had taken up employment at a local bakery and had struck up a relationship with the son of the business. She had confided to her admirer that the child was hers and that her own father had fathered the baby. The baker had reported this to the local officer Peter Pinder. PC Pinder had checked with the girl and rung the CID office. Incest was a CID matter. PC Pinder also said that he believed that the father was aware of the police interest and that he had been told that the father had all the family in the house and that he may have a gun.

These were the days before armed police, negotiators and SWAT (skill with arms tactical) teams. I told PC Pinder that he should go to the house and that Dick Leach and I would meet him there.

We arrived at the house and as we walked to the front gate we were greeted by a shotgun waving from the first floor bedroom window and the father shouting, 'Come any nearer and I'll shoot you.'

25

I said, 'Now come on, you know us, we only want to talk to you.'

He yelled, 'Go away or I'll shoot.'

Dick responded, 'Don't be silly, it's not that serious.'

'It is,' replied the man. 'I'll go to prison, now go away or I'll shoot you.'

We withdrew out of sight and decided on a plan. We summoned other CID colleagues and decided that we would occupy the father by talking to him whilst PC Pinder and the other officers got the family out through the back.

The talking began and as it was clear that the father knew exactly why we wanted him and that he was facing lengthy imprisonment, we realised that we would not be able to fool him into giving himself up. It appeared that we were in for a long siege, which would not be a problem if the family were out of the house. We were attracting a lot of attention from police officers with little to do on a quiet afternoon. The radio traffic brought motor patrol and beat officers.

The father suddenly said, 'If any more police come, I'll shoot myself.'

We thought this was a considerable improvement on him shooting us, but almost immediately a big white police motorcycle turned into the road. Bang! from the first floor. Dick and I ran in. Upstairs, a door banged and we threw ourselves down thinking it was another shot.

In the bedroom we found the father, still alive, with a severe wound in his upper chest from the shotgun lying near him. We removed the gun and applied a pillow as a pressure bandage. An ambulance had been called and we gave artificial respiration while awaiting its arrival. The man was taken to the Hospital of St Cross where Dick and I followed shortly afterwards.

In casualty we saw the doctor and asked how the patient was progressing. 'Dead,' said the doctor.

We said that we were not surprised as the wound was severe.

'Oh no,' said the doctor, 'he had lost all his blood, some-body had pumped it out of him.'

We were dismayed that our first aid had killed him.

'It's OK,' said the doctor, 'he would have died anyway – you just speeded it up.'

There were no counsellors in those days, so we went to the police club!

PC Bill Corder, whose leg was broken when we were both on the beat, was still on shifts but always hankering for a place in the traffic department. He was not noted for his industry, but had an impressive spell when 'showing round' a young probationer, Gerry McCullough. It was Gerry's first tour of night duty and Bill was showing him the property to be checked. They were down a very long and dark alley at the back of shops in High Street not long after 10pm when they found the rear door of Greys Sports shop forced open. Bill left Gerry to guard the door whilst he went to telephone for a key-holder. The obvious phone was in the Three Horse Shoes Hotel, two streets away! Bill rang the police station to call out a key-holder, had a pint and wandered back to Gerry who was trying to restrain three burglars who had been inside the shop. All were arrested and of course, Bill's story was somewhat different to the true one. This began a series of events where Bill could do no wrong. He and Gerry had pris-oners on most nights of their tour. Easy for Bill, as crime prisoners were dealt with by CID. Bill had only to supply the statement of arrest.

The final incident came when they moved to the 2pm–10pm shift. Once again Bill and Gerry were on duty in the town centre. Bill rang the police station to check a suspi-cious vehicle and found that it was stolen. The vehicle was parked in the square by the clock tower. I was dispatched to assist. I arrived in the CID car to find the stolen car parked with two men in it and Bill standing with Gerry, one either side of the car. I asked Bill what the men had said.

Bill said, 'Nothing, I was waiting for you.'

I went to the car and saw two mature men.

'CID,' I announced. 'What are you doing here?'

With that they were out and off. One produced a crowbar and started waving it about. I grabbed him and he hit me on the arm with the crowbar. Gerry was waving ineffectively at him with his truncheon and the man made off again, with us in pursuit. He kept swinging at us with the bar and we could not get near him. The pursuit continued and I managed to knock his ankles together with a kick. He fell over and then sat up waving the iron bar at me. I kicked him on the forearm – and this time he didn't get up. I arrested him and went back to the car where Bill had detained the second man with the assistance of other officers.

Both men were taken to the police station and the vehicle searched. There was a .22 revolver and ammunition in the car. We had all escaped lightly! The two men were from Leamington Spa, professional burglars intending to commit crime in Rugby when Bill spotted them.

I charged the men with 'assault with intent to resist arrest and possession of part 1 firearm and ammunition' . The first charge enabled us to commit the men to trial at quarter sessions where they were both sentenced to substantial prison terms. We told Bill Corder to go back to his less industrious mode, it was safer.

During my time in the CID at Rugby personnel changed and in particular the Detective Inspector. The new man was not of the same calibre as his predecessor. Discontent led to reduced performance. Scapegoats were found and transfers began. I could see that I would soon be in the firing line for a move and decided on a pre-emptive strike. I had been married in December 1965 and it was some twelve months later that I deceitfully used my wife to engineer a move to Nuneaton, saying, 'She would like to be nearer home.' Doreen agreed to this and backed me up in my subterfuge. I am sure my ploy was recognised for I was soon transferred to Nuneaton but in uniform not CID! However, it turned out to be an excellent move which set me on the path to a successful career.

Chapter Four

Back Home

Nuneaton. My home town, industry and coal. Plenty of crime and busier all round than Rugby. I was in uniform, back on shifts. I was looked on with some suspicion at first as it was a demotion to be returned to uniform from CID. The suspicion did not last long and I was fully accepted. The work was steady but unchallenging and I soon began to look for a return to CID. I was diverted by the introduction of The Unit Beat System, known to the public as 'panda cars'.

A successful experiment in Lancashire had been followed by the introduction of the system throughout the country. We were not to know it, but pandas were to lead to the loss of public confidence due to the lack of contact between police and public, other than in confrontational situations, and the removal of foot patrols due to the need to keep the cars fully manned. (Hindsight: I have a degree in it, as have most people.)

In 1967 however, there was great excitement. A fleet of blue and white Minis arrived and a group picture was taken for the local press. The system was very simple. Each beat was allocated a resident officer working his own hours, according to the demands of the beat. Two adjacent beats became a unit covered by a panda car on twenty-four-hour cover. The resident officers had a bicycle and were to develop a liaison with their local population. The cars were

29

to be parked conspicuously and the drivers patrol on foot nearby. All officers carried personal radios and were supported by a collator who collected and disseminated information and intelligence, the theory being that movement of officers would not result in a loss of local knowledge.

I was allocated a resident beat. It was semi-rural: I covered the affluent side of town, the local barracks at Bramcote and twenty-eight farms. The early days were very successful and enjoyable. I developed an excellent working relationship with the neighbouring beat officer, Ivan Milbourne, we took great delight when working 6pm to 2am at weekends in cycling at great speed to arrive at incidents before the panda car.

The job of resident beat officer was a blank sheet and offered great scope for work or idleness. In addition to the self-created work, enquiries from other divisions or police forces were allocated to the resident officer as were minor crimes and other complaints not requiring urgent attention. Two memorable incidents involved dogs.

I was somewhat wary of dogs due to incidents in my childhood and my experience with police dogs. One day I received a warrant for the arrest of a lady on my beat. The warrant was issued by the Metropolitan Police for non-payment of parking fines. I thought this was somewhat draconian but I was duty bound to execute the warrant. The house was a large detached residence. I knocked and was admitted. I told the lady of the house the situation: she laughed and implied that she thought I was joking. I told her that I was in earnest. Whilst talking to her I could hear the barking of a large dog. The lady shouted, 'Be quiet Sebastian!'

A large name for a large dog I thought. I asked the lady whether she had the money to pay the amount owed. Before she could answer, a door burst open and in came what appeared to be a black and white pony. It rushed at me and put its forelegs on my shoulders and thankfully started licking me. I nearly died; it was a Harlequin Great Dane. The dog was removed and my resolve to arrest the lady unless cash was forthcoming vanished. I said, 'Send a cheque and I'll come back in a week to see the receipt.'

I left. Discretion is allowed in some cases.

The second dog incident was an enquiry following a complaint from a postman that he had been bitten by a boxer dog whilst delivering mail. I called at the house and followed the normal routine which was to acquaint the owners with the complaint, obtain their version of events and then call for the dog to be brought in to observe and note its demeanour. Everything went well: the dog was friendly, and I even took tea whilst talking to the owners. 'Well,' I explained, 'you will have to be reported, but I don't see a lot of difficulty – the dog is very well behaved. It's strange, some dogs just don't like uniform or hats.'

With that I put my helmet on and the dog bit me!

I said, 'You will be reported for that as well,' and left.

It soon became obvious that any shortage of panda car drivers was made up by taking the resident officers from their beats. This was fine for variety of work but no good whatsoever for continuity in fostering good relationships. My desire for CID returned. It was not an easy task as there was always a waiting list. It was necessary to get yourself noticed for the right reasons. I did this by becoming a willing horse, not refusing work or unusual duties. It eventually paid off when I was selected to become the Divisional Crime Intelligence Officer, a new post and therefore another blank sheet of paper. It turned out to be a dual role. I was nominally an operational Detective with a special responsibility for Crime Intelligence.

The CID at Nuneaton was a larger establishment than at Rugby. We had a DCI and a DI but the department was run by the Detective Sergeant, Ken James. He considered himself 'as pure as the driven snow'. I doubted that, but he was certainly a man of great integrity and absolutely committed to the detection of crime and conviction of criminals. He was to show later his complete abhorrence of any element of police corruption.

The work was varied, as were the staff. I became particularly friendly with Michael John Regan – his behaviour was eccentric but often hilariously funny. Our DI had come from Force Headquarters on promotion from Scenes of Crime Department. Scene examination was in its infancy as we generally carried out our own finger-printing and photography. The variability of results led to the specialisation of certain officers to ensure maximum benefit from the evidence available at scenes of serious crime. The minor matters were left to us.

A break-in had occurred at the local flour mill, and money and property had been stolen. Mick Regan was the investigating officer. He had made an arrest and was strongly advised by our DI, Fred Price, to take the prisoners' clothing and send it for forensic examination. The DI was always preaching at us about proper packaging and handling of exhibits. Mick was instructed to lay out the clothing on brown paper sheets and pack them securely. The DI said that the laboratory would be sure to find traces of flour which would secure a conviction. Mick was instructed to call for the DI when he had completed the task.

The DI was called for and shown a pair of trousers, a sweater, shirt, socks and underclothes laid out on individual sheets on brown paper on the office floor. We were not too aware of the problems of cross contamination in those days.

The DI said, 'Wrap them up, don't leave them there.'

Mick said, 'Just a minute sir,' and pulled a small bag of flour from his desk drawer and began to sprinkle it all over the clothing.

The DI went absolutely crazy and said, 'What are you doing?'

'You said the lab would find some flour on the clothes. They will now.' The DI was speechless until Mick said, 'It's all right sir. These aren't his clothes, they are some old ones from the cupboard.'

Fred Price did not see the funny side of the joke at all and Mick was summoned to his office for a lengthy lecture.

Mick and I were called one morning to a burglary at James Motorcycle showroom and workshops at Abbey Green, Nuneaton. The property was very old and entry had been gained through a front upstairs window reached from an adjacent roof. Abbey Green was a busy shopping area on the edge of town. We had taken the fingerprint kit with us and Mick began to 'dust' the window and frame for fingerprints. However, the frame was rotten, and the whole thing, frame and glass, fell out. It was gone before we could grab it. We looked out to see it spinning down to the street. We called out but it was too late. The frame hit a man squarely on his head and settled on his shoulders. We ran downstairs into the street to find the man running about like the proverbial headless chicken. He was bleeding profusely from the head. No-one knew what had happened but a crowd had gathered.

Mick called out the classic words, 'Stand back, I'm a first-aider.'

We got hold of the man and calmed him down, but it was clear that the frame could not be removed without causing further injury. The town hospital was some 400 yards away and we decided to take him to casualty. Mick got the first aid kit but there was little we could do but drape a triangular bandage round his neck.

The next problem was getting him into the car. Eventually we had him three quarters in the car with his head and the window-frame outside. I had to hold the door through the open window whilst Mick drove to the hospital.

At the hospital, we took his details and sent someone to fetch his wife. We had not told anyone what had occurred. It was obvious. The window was removed and the nurses were cleaning him up when his wife arrived. She was told by the staff that her husband had fallen through a window. She immediately castigated him for being drunk and further berated him about the whereabouts of the washing he was supposed to be taking to the launderette. We thought that there would be less trouble if we left things as they were. I am sure that the poor man never knew how he came to have a window round his neck. His injuries were fortunately only superficial and thankfully these were the days before compensation claims.

Chapter Five

Murder

I had during my boyhood associated the word 'detective' with the word 'murder' and eagerly awaited my first murder investigation, with no thought that someone had to die violently for this to occur. There had been no murders in Warwickshire since I joined and there was great excitement when we heard that the naked body of a young woman had been found in Bickenhill Lane, Elmdon which was not far from the Birmingham City boundary but was in Warwickshire. A murder investigation had begun based at Hobs Moat Police Station, Solihull. I and another Nuneaton officer were selected to assist and we set off in high excitement for our first murder.

The unfortunate victim was Sylvia Whitehouse, a young Birmingham girl who had last been seen alive at a bus stop outside Smallheath bus garage. The investigation was complicated by the body having been found in Warwickshire and the disappearance having occurred in Birmingham. There was no expertise whatsoever in murder investigation and it was necessary to 'call in the yard'. This was to ask for assistance from the Metropolitan Police who would send a Detective Chief Superintendent and a Detective Sergeant from C1 at New Scotland Yard to lead the investigation.

My role was totally insignificant. My colleague and I were given routine, but necessary, enquiries on the periphery of the investigation but we were present at the daily briefings when the great man from the yard told us of progress and plans. There were a great number of officers involved in the enquiry including many officers engaged in searching a refuse tip in Arelwas in Staffordshire for Sylvia's shoes and other belongings.

There was an early suspect and both enquiries and the tip search pointed to him. Anthony Ian Hall was arrested and later convicted of this particularly vicious murder.

This first murder in many years was quickly followed by an apparently motiveless murder at Henley-in-Arden, a picturesque market town between Birmingham and Stratford-on-Avon. A mature lady had been walking across 'The Mount', the site of an old castle, to work one morning around 8am when she was strangled. There was great consternation in the town that such a brutal and mindless act could take place in such an idyllic location.

Once again 'The Yard' were called and I was selected with Mick Regan from Nuneaton. The incident room was established in the Parish Hall at Beaudesert Lane. Mick and I knew that we were too inexperienced to be given 'live' enquiries, but were pleased to be part of the investigation.

We were to be part of a team of officers who were to descend on the factory where the deceased was employed in an administrative position. Family and work colleagues were an obvious area for first suspicions and it was intended that everyone at her workplace would be interviewed on the first day.

We were gathered in a group to be briefed by our leader. He said, 'My name is Shaw, Inspector Shaw. I am not a Detective Inspector. Yet.' Mick and I exchanged knowing nods. Inspector Shaw told us where we were going and what we were going to do. He then said, 'When you take statements from the staff, I want you to put their names and addresses at the top.'

Mick turned to me and said, 'He's good. Soon be a DI.'

I laughed and the Inspector said, 'You, talking, what's your name?'

36

'Regan,' said Mick.

'I'll remember you,' said Mr Shaw.

When we got to the factory, we all assembled in the Managing Director's office where Inspector Shaw sat next to the Managing Director's desk. He went through his briefing again in front of the Managing Director, including the 'names and addresses at the top of the statements' innovation. Mick and I exchanged smiles which did not go unnoticed.

The Inspector began to allocate areas to pairs of detectives. 'Hannis and Recan, it is Recan is it?' knowing well that it was not.

'No sir,' said Mick grandly, 'Regan, you've probably heard of us, the hunting Regans of County Mayo.'

I knew then that Mick and I were in for a difficult murder. I was right.

We were given lots of house-to-house enquiries and as this was a very rural area we were visiting isolated farms and houses and working long hours. The enquiry was getting nowhere. The strategy at that time was to throw massive resources, especially manpower, at the enquiry in the early days. The murder was declared a 'special occasion' which allowed all overtime to be paid and we were all earning a lot of money. The maximum length of this special occasion was to be fourteen days and it was important to have it resolved by the end of this period. As a force we were novices in murder investigations but were well aware that if there was no potential in the first two or three days, then it would be a struggle. So it proved in this case. The victim had led a blameless life, there were no suspects and no witnesses, and the location was extremely isolated and little-used at that early hour of the morning.

The house-to-house enquiries were extended to further afield. The purpose of these home visits was twofold: firstly to seek information which might assist the enquiry and secondly to eliminate the male members of the household by establishing their whereabouts at the crucial time.

37

There was no positive evidence that the offender was male, but all instincts supported this view.

Mick Regan had a wicked sense of humour and we made the best of our time by lightening the day where possible. This often took the form of story telling when visiting houses for our enquiries. We would regale the occupants with stories of our prowess as detectives and our self-sacrifice and devotion to duty. This always resulted in at least tea and cakes and sometimes something stronger. One evening we knocked at the door of a large country house and were greeted with the question 'Are you Tories?'

When we identified ourselves and our purpose, we readily declared our allegiance to the Conservative party and were invited in. The homeowner and his wife had spent the day in London and brought back some goodies for supper. Michael and I were soon ensconced in an armchair with a glass of scotch and a large portion of pork pie each. We were well into the second week of the enquiry and were in no hurry. We did our usual double act and also managed to fill in the necessary forms whilst our generous host kept our glasses topped up. He was very interested in the enquiry and our place in it. We discussed with him the need for improvements in equipment and conditions. We knew from our form-filling that our host was a man of property and influence, but saw no danger in our indiscretions; we were all having rather a nice evening.

It came time to leave and our host said, 'I found that all very interesting, I shall mention it to the local chap, Dick.'

'Dick?' I said. 'No Sir, the local man is John, PC John Smith.'

'No, not him, Matthews,' said our host.

'You mean, the Chief, Richard Matthews?' said Mick.

'Yes, good chap Dick, he will be very interested in your views.'

'No no, I'm sure he won't want to know about us,' I said, sensing disaster ahead.

'Well, I'll write to Eric then,' said our new friend.

'Eric? You mean Eric Watson the ACC?' I said weakly.

'No, Eric St Johnson.'

Mick said, 'But he is Her Majesty's Chief Inspector.'

'I know that, good friend of mine,' replied our friend.

We left hoping that it was whisky talking and that it would all be forgotten in the morning. Not so!

Mick and I were driving into Stratford one morning to call at the office of Flowers Brewery for a routine enquiry. We had become the 'official' brewery detectives and fielded all enquiries relating to their employees. We had visited so often we were now in receipt of two pints of beer each visit, our allowance. We passed two young ladies hitch-hiking who had Swiss flags on their rucksacks. We stopped and offered a lift into Stratford which they accepted. We dropped them off and went to the Flowers office. Our next call was on the other side of town and there were the two girls again. We knew that they were heading for the Cotswolds and as we had nearly completed our day's work allotment, we offered to drive them to Broadway. We had a pleasant hour or so showing them the villages on the way and when we dropped them off we presented each of them with a signed murder poster as a souvenir. We often wondered what their parents thought when they returned to Switzerland with their macabre memento.

The enquiry was now beginning to drag and as the devil makes work for idle hands we were quite likely to fall seriously foul of our leader Inspector Shaw. We were somewhat relieved therefore when a vagrant who had been arrested in Evesham for a minor matter readily confessed to the Henley murder. It was the fourteenth day of the special occasion – some cynics suggested that the Crime Squad had paid him to lie low until the last day of the overtime money.

The victim had been the subject of a robbery by a passing vagrant on her way to work. An unbelievable occurrence in Shakespeare's Arden.

A few weeks later Mick and I had resumed duties at

Nuneaton when we were summoned to the office by our DCI, John Ashmead.

'What have you two been up to now?' he asked, answering his own question by producing a letter from our friend with the whisky and pork pie. He had written to the Chief commending our 'selfless devotion to duty' and suggesting various changes in pay and allowances as well as advocating the greater use of helicopters in murder enquiries. The Chief Constable had instructed that we be seen and advised that any future ideas for the improvement of the force be forwarded to him rather than to a senior member of the Conservative party. We left suitably chastised.

Sadly, murders began to increase in frequency and it was not too long until provincial Forces dispensed with assistance from New Scotland Yard. Murder investigation was the application of a system, there was no Sherlock Holmes element, it was dogged police work, although there was always room for innovation and daring.

I had been seconded to a number of murder investigations during my later secondment to the Regional Crime Squad and as an 'elite' we were fortunate to be allocated 'live' enquiries relating to serious suspects. On my subsequent return to divisional duties at Coventry, I became something of an expert in running house-to-house enquiries. These were tedious but essential enquiries and even more so when the scene and the victim's address were within a densely populated area. The first task in house to house was to decide with the Senior Investigating Officer the primary area to be covered and then to design the pro forma to be used. The job then was to supervise the officers carrying out the enquiries directing and collating the results.

My job was to ensure that each address was visited, every occupant seen, and that those of an age and description fitting into the profile of a potential suspect be eliminated as far as possible from the enquiry. Cross checking of pro formas assisted in this elimination by neighbours verifying others' whereabouts.

There was one murder enquiry where I found it puzzling that the occupants of a small block of flats were all doing the same thing at the relevant time and all watching the same television programme, which was not a soap. I brought this up and we found that the officers concerned, a young policewoman and older male officer had been engaged in other activities in their car, and had filled in all the forms themselves without visiting the addresses to give more time for their canoodling. They were removed from the enquiry and all their work handed to others. They were very unpopular – they had made extra work and could have let the offender escape justice.

Putting men and women in close proximity has always caused, and will always cause, problems from time to time. I am reminded of a time, much later in my service, at a Chief Superintendent's conference that the difficulty caused by police men and women having affairs came up for discussion. There were serious discussions about associations forming on patrol and intercourse taking place in the police car on nights. Bob Mills, an old friend from Rugby days, was clearly bemused by the extent of the discussion and decided to terminate it. He said, 'I have studied this subject and have decided that providing they keep their hats on and they are not smoking, there is nothing we can do about it.'

The room dissolved into laughter and we moved on to more serious matters.

Innovation and daring were well illustrated by the investigation into the murder of Peter Blakemore, a newspaper delivery boy who was abducted and murdered during his morning paper round in the streets adjacent to Coventry City Football Ground.

The boy had been reported missing after failing to return from his paper round one morning. Enquiries had begun, but a full-scale search had not been instigated when the poor boy's naked body was found lying in a back alleyway of some terraced houses.

The Senior Investigating Officer was to be Alf Horrobin, with whom I later had a run-in over the body of a baby in a dustbin. I was put in charge of house-to-house and we agreed an area to include some seven hundred houses, the majority terraced properties.

It was very promising in the early stages, in that the boy had disappeared part way through his round. The first enquiry was, 'How far had he got?' For then, Alf would know from where he was abducted. This was soon established and enquiries concentrated on the houses in that area.

The boy was naked when found and had a strange pattern of post-mortem staining on his back. There were obviously indications to be gleaned by both pathologist and forensic scientists from the body, but the boy's clothes and his paper-bag with the remaining newspapers were missing.

The senior investigating officer (SIO) decided to examine the contents of every dustbin in the house-to-house search area. He arranged this through the council by using an empty vehicle to collect all refuse in the house-to-house area on the normal collection day. No warning was given and officers labelled each collection for future reference. The search resulted in the recovery of several items from different addresses. Someone was being very clever.

The scientists came up with a very interesting result from an examination of the fibres found on the body and the pattern of the post-mortem staining. They were able to say that after death, the boy had lain on a candlewick bedspread of a particular colour and pattern. They were also able to specify the colours of the blankets, sheets and carpet in the room where he had lain. This was extraordinary and all officers were shown the unique combination of colours at morning briefing.

A large number of the seven hundred plus houses had been visited by the house-to-house teams and in order to eliminate them there would now need to be a second visit. The SIO then decided on a bold and, at that time, unique approach. It was essential that all the houses in the specific

42

area were searched for the colour combination and in the normal course of events this would take many days. The SIO decided to do them all in one day!

He had the forensic science laboratory produce a sample of the colours and materials in the room where the body had lain. This sample was issued to each pair of officers. Each pair were allocated a block of houses which they were to visit and where there was any likelihood of a match with the sample, they were to seize the bedding, bag it, and take it to the local pub by the Coventry City Ground where the SIO had installed the scientists with their equipment in the function room. The materials seized would be examined and eliminated there and then. Brilliant, expensive and what would the public think!

The day selected was a Sunday – most people would be in and we were to start at 9am. There was no search warrant, but goodwill only. We were instructed to guarantee an amnesty on any items found related to minor crimes in order to guarantee co-operation. In the event, people were marvellous and readily allowed officers to tramp through their houses. This was as a result of the genuine concern of the neighbourhood to solve this dreadful crime.

It worked like a charm and at about 11.30am the scientists said 'this is it'. A team was despatched to search the address and to detain the occupants. The house was then minutely examined by scientists.

A young male occupant of the house later admitted the murder. He had decided 'to kill somebody'. He saw the paper boy, enticed him into the house and killed him. A completely random and motiveless attack detected by a bold and intelligent detective.

Chapter Six

'George' and Promotion

I had succeeded in passing my promotion examination to Sergeant during these early days of my career at Nuneaton. I felt that although only 26 years of age, I had a very good chance of being successful in the forthcoming round of promotion boards in 1969. The system at this time was that your own Chief Superintendent wrote an assessment of you and this was followed by an interview before a promotion board chaired by an Assistant Chief Constable. There were nine members of the board in total, all Chief Superintendents and Superintendents. At the conclusion of each candidate's interview, there was a show of hands as to the candidate's suitability for promotion. The candidates with nine votes were the first to be promoted and then eight votes and so on until all the vacancies were filled. We knew that there were to be a lot of promotions following the current round of promotion boards as Warwickshire was to amalgamate with Coventry City in November of that year.

The boards were a travelling event and were convened at the Divisional Police Stations around the county.

The interview was a traumatic experience, for a board of nine is far too big. I can only remember one question and that was a leading one from the Chairman, Assistant Chief Constable, Eric Watson. He asked me to confirm that I had cultivated Bill Corder's allotment when he had been assaulted and injured some years previously. I confirmed this and could see a lot of appreciative nods around the table. I came out feeling quietly confident. The results of the boards were not published: you only became aware of your success or failure when the list of those being called for promotion was telexed around the force.

Detectives are resourceful however. We knew that the Chief Superintendent kept the notes he made at the interviews in a locked desk drawer. The lock was an FS series as used in car ignitions. A colleague and I took the lock number one evening and bought a key from a garage the following day. That evening we again entered the Chief Superintendent's unlocked office and opened his drawer. We found the notes and saw that I had the magic nine votes but sadly my colleague had only one. I was also able to read my assessment which was good and suggested that I would probably make the rank of Inspector.

My expedition had resulted in my knowing that I would certainly be promoted to Sergeant at the forthcoming amalgamation. I was in a very strong position to be able to manipulate this to my advantage by virtually selecting my own post. I intended to become a Detective Sergeant on the Regional Crime Squad. This would be a great achievement at seven-and-a-half years' service. The ability to do this had come purely by chance and was a turning point in my career and subsequently nearly my downfall. A telephone call which I happened to answer led to my involvement in one of the most serious and far reaching police corruption enquiries ever to have taken place.

One Monday morning in early autumn (24 September 1969), it was reported that a break-in had occurred at the Co-operative supermarket in Abbey Street in Nuneaton town centre and that their complete stock of cigarettes had been stolen.

The first detectives at the scene and the Scenes of Crime Officer were unable to discover a point of entry. We usually fell back on the 'duplicate key' method when this occurred but in this case there were no obvious suspects.

45

The amount involved was very large for a shop break-in in a provincial town. Detective Sergeant James took charge and organised thorough enquiries.

Witnesses were found who saw men in white coats loading a van parked in the street shortly after closing time on the previous Saturday. It was daylight and very busy as the normal Saturday street market was being cleared. The activity of the men attracted no attention whatsoever. It began to appear that the 'duplicate key' theory was highly feasible.

Enquiries with the Regional Criminal records offices and C9 department at New Scotland Yard, the office responsible for provincial liaison, revealed that there was currently a spate of duplicate key shop break-ins. The areas of operation were the South East, Home Counties and more recently the Midlands. This information led to the conclusion that this was a 'London job' and we were therefore going to be in some difficulty in detecting the crime.

Late the same Monday afternoon a telephone call was received from the police at Peckham in south-east London. They had found a van loaded with boxes of cigarettes labelled 'Nuneaton CWS' and the officer enquired whether we had 'lost any'. DS James was called to the telephone and asked the uniform Sergeant at Peckham whether he had informed the local CID.

'Not likely,' he said. 'They'll go missing!'

DS James had previously had dealings with CID officers from the Metropolitan Police whose honesty he had doubted. He instructed the Peckham officer to hang on to the van and he would travel down to London. Approval was sought and given for him and DC Jack Wilson to travel to London to pursue enquiries. They left immediately.

The following morning we were informed that DS James had formed a good working relationship with the local CID at Peckham and that arrests were highly likely. The stolen property was completely intact. There was general delight at what looked like a very good result on a difficult case.

In the afternoon of that Tuesday I answered a telephone call in the CID office. The caller was a male with a southern accent.

He said, 'I know where your cigarettes are.'

'What cigarettes?'

'From the Co-op.'

I then said, 'I know where they are as well, but how do you know?'

The caller said, 'I know who did it and how they got in.'

'What do you want?' I asked.

The man replied, 'I want paying.'

I asked him who he was and where he was, but he refused to give me any information. I asked whether we could meet and he agreed to do so.

The man arranged a meeting outside the Hippodrome Theatre in Coventry later that afternoon.

He said, 'I'm only a little bloke, I'll be in a grey suit and carrying a *Telegraph* under my arm.'

We arranged a time and I hastily sought permission from the DCI. I took another DC with me as backup.

The man was there as arranged. We went to a café and I asked him questions about the offence. It was clear that he was genuine and that he knew a great deal about the team who were carrying out the duplicate key shop break-ins. It was also obvious that he must in some way be involved. I thought it likely that he had missed out on his share of the proceeds. I asked him for names of those involved and he gave me two names, Roy Brooks and Michael Perry. I insisted on his full name and date of birth before we could proceed further. He willingly gave me those details but refused his address until he knew that we were to be trusted. I decided to give him a cover name and from that day on he was 'George'.

We took George to Nuneaton police station and I then spoke to DS James in London. I told him what had occurred and what had been said. DS James was very excited and said, 'I've got Roy Brooks locked up here. This George

47

knows what he's talking about, bring him down.'

George agreed to travel and I took him to London accompanied by another officer. We talked a great deal on the way. He was very amiable and very knowledgeable. The duplicate key team mainly concentrated on premises with glass doors as they were in possession of a large number of master keys for different suites of locks by several manufacturers. The main target was clothing which was easily disposed of. George was able to give an address for Perry and willing to point out other addresses.

We were keen to protect George and his identity and did not wish him to be seen by Metropolitan officers. I arranged to meet DS James and DC Wilson away from Peckham police station. The meeting was very fruitful and it was decided to pursue enquiries the following morning. George said that he would stop with his mother overnight. We gave him some money and we booked into a Police Section House for the night.

DS James updated us with his progress to date. The DI at Peckham, Mr Sylvester, had been very helpful and assigned officers to assist. It was well known that Roy Brooks was involved in duplicate key shop breaking and local information pointed to his having been involved in our Co-op break in. He had been arrested and was lodged at Peckham. DS James had intended to take him back to Nuneaton that day but had delayed this as a result of my telephone call. The intention was now to find Perry, arrest him and take both him and Brooks back to Nuneaton.

The following morning we met George and were taken to an address where Perry lived above a newspaper shop in Camberwell. George also pointed out other likely addresses of other members of the team. We dropped George off and arranged a rendezvous for later that day. We were aware by this time of George's criminal record of theft and burglaries over a number of years. He did not attempt to deny any of this.

DS James had been given the name of a DS Symonds at

Camberwell who would assist with Perry. We met the DS who was helpful, but treated us a bit like country bumpkins, which I suppose we were. He said it was unlikely that Perry was involved with our offence but he would help us find him. Perry was at the address and was arrested. There was nothing to incriminate him at the flat and he refused to say anything. Perry was taken to Camberwell police station and lodged in the cells. We, the provincial officers, left Perry there and went off to further debrief George. We were anxious to gain as much information as possible about both Brooks' and Perry's involvement in order to support our interrogation. Satisfied that we had all information we returned to Camberwell. George had said that he would remain in London, but would contact me at Nuneaton when he returned. I was happy with that as we had struck up a good relationship. It was agreed that I would be his future contact which turned out to be something of a poisoned chalice.

The plan now was for my colleague and I to take Perry from Camberwell and join DS James at Peckham where he would collect Brooks. We would then all travel back to Nuneaton together in two cars.

DS Symonds at Camberwell was very friendly. He assisted with signing out Perry, having first told me that he did not think that Perry was guilty. Symonds then qualified this by stating that Perry would not admit anything in any case. I told Symonds that we had the right men in Perry and Brooks. We said our farewells and assured Symonds that we would keep in touch.

I drove Perry to Peckham where we were met in the station yard by DS James. He told us that Brooks had escaped from the cells. We were incredulous, as was DS James. He related to us that on arrival at Peckham, he was greeted by a scene of confusion, there were uniformed and CID officers milling about. The DI, Sylvester, told DS James that Brooks had attacked the jailer and escaped. The DI indicated a uniform officer who appeared to have blood on his face and uniform. Ken James expressed his concern, but was told that it was not blood but tomatoes. Brooks had thrown his meal at the jailer, pushed past him and run off. DS James asked the pertinent question as to how he was able to escape from the cell block and was told that it had been left unlocked! He also discovered that Brooks had managed to take his property with him which included several hundred pounds in cash. There was obviously a grave problem and more than a suspicion of a corrupt act by one or more of the Peckham officers. Ken James expressed his displeasure but was assured that Brooks would soon be recaptured.

Having related his story DS James instructed me to take Perry back to Nuneaton forthwith. He and Jack Wilson would remain and endeavour to recover Brooks.

We drove Perry to Nuneaton. This was an excellent opportunity to interrogate him. Perry was friendly and chatty, but denied all knowledge of the Co-op burglary and the activities of the duplicate key team. The questioning continued on a more formal basis at Nuneaton police station, but with no result. Perry was firm in his resolve to deny the offence.

Perry was detained overnight. During the next day Ken James returned from London empty-handed. Further interviews took place with Perry in which we intimated that we had witnesses and fingerprint evidence, all to no avail. Eventually Perry said, 'Look, you are wasting your time. I know you've got nothing. No witnesses. No fingerprints, just someone putting my name in. You might just as well let me go.'

I said, 'How can you know?'

Perry said, 'I know. I'll have to pay when I get back.'

'Pay who?'

'The one that told me you have got nothing.'

'Who is that?' I said hopefully.

'I'm not telling you, but it will cost me when I get back.'

The questioning continued for a while but with the same answers.

I informed DS James of the situation which he confirmed by talking to Perry. A conference ensued at which we all agreed that Perry would have to be released.

Perry was bailed to re-appear in some weeks' time.

Within a day or so of Perry's release, Peckham were in touch with DS James to say that Brooks had given himself up and that he was accompanied by a magistrate, who was prepared to say that Brooks had been with him at 6pm the previous Saturday night, the time of the Co-op burglary. There was no point in travelling to London to bring Brooks back to Nuneaton. It was agreed that he would be bailed from Peckham.

It was clear that we were involved in some extremely dishonest police activity. We knew from past experience that there was little point in pursuing a complaint within the Metropolitan Police – it would come to nothing.

Enquiries were continued at the Nuneaton end in an effort to produce some physical evidence and contact was resumed with George to see if he could assist further. Contact was maintained with C9 at New Scotland Yard and established with various Regional Crime Squad Offices who were dealing with duplicate key shop break-ins.

We began to form something of a picture that involved many burglaries around the country and I began to come under pressure to hand over my informant, George. I was visited by DCI McGrory from the Leicester crime squad office, a very powerful personality. I resisted all his cajoling and threats to disclose George's identity and address. I had by now found out the result of my promotion board and knew that if I played my cards right that I would get promoted on to the Regional Crime Squad.

The overtures continued from Leicester reinforced by efforts from Coventry and Birmingham, but I stood my ground.

Throughout this whole period DS Symonds kept in regular touch. We had no suspicion regarding him and found him to be very helpful.

At last the great day came. I was summoned with many others to police headquarters at Leek Wootton. I was ushered into the office of Chief Constable Richard Matthews.

We were given a short lecture on the responsibilities of rank and the importance of the success of the amalgamation with Coventry. The Chief then read out the list of promotions. 'DC202 Hannis to Detective Sergeant number 4 Regional Crime Squad, Coventry office.' I was elated.

I decided to call into the Coventry office on my way back to Nuneaton. I knew the DI, Barry Kirton, from my days at Rugby, but I did not know the DCI, John Crapper.

I walked into the office and announced to the DI and DCI, 'I've just been promoted and I'm coming here next week.'

The DI said, 'And you are to bring your informant with you and you are both going to London.'

Chapter Seven

'Coathanger' and
The Times

Clearly there had been much discussion during the preceding weeks. George had continued to supply information on personalities which I had passed on. The information was obviously accurate for now the plan was to base him in London and actively involve him with the duplicate key team. The usual caution against acting as 'agent provocateur' and active participation in burglaries was given and was to be enforced.

I learned during the ensuing few days before my promotion that I was to become a part of 'Operation Coathanger', established to combat the activities of the duplicate key team. The operation was based at New Scotland Yard in C9 department and was made up of officers from a number of Regional Crime Squads: numbers 4, 6 and 9. The officers were a DS and DC from Leicester, myself and a DC from Coventry, a DS and a WDS from Maidstone and a DS from Brighton. There were also other officers but they were to be in a more peripheral role. The team was to be run on a daily basis, by a DI from the Metropolitan Police posted to C9 and overseen by a DCI from Maidstone.

At this stage, I did not know any of the officers at all, not even my own DC.

George was still something of a shadowy figure. He was a Londoner from south of the river. He was a thief, but not a villain in so much as there was no violence in him. He was a cunning, personable minor criminal with an ability to blend in to any scenario. George was living in the Nuneaton area having been brought there by work which he was obliged to take to keep himself out of custody. His heart was in London and he readily accepted the offer to take him to London and run him against the duplicate key team. His motive at this time was not clear, but I thought it was revenge for being cut out of the proceeds of the Co-op burglary. As we progressed, it became clear that he enjoyed it.

Money was important for George. He would be able to pay his wife and support himself with the figure that we agreed, both parties accepting that George would no doubt make money from his involvement with the duplicate key team.

It was necessary for George to be introduced to DI Barry Kirton before the operation began in order that he could stress the necessity for George to avoid direct involvement in burglaries, to assure him of our support and the protection of his identity. He was told that he would need to meet the DI from C9 but that otherwise his dealings would solely be with me and my DC, Ken Brown. It was agreed that George would travel to London alone and I would meet him when I had settled in and been fully briefed.

I had told my wife that I would be going to London for an unspecified period. I was to be picked up from home and taken to Coventry to meet my DC and be given my car and further instructions.

On the Wednesday morning of my promotion I was taken to Coventry and introduced to my DC. It was clear from the outset that he thought he should have my job. It was also clear that he thought that I was naïve and inexperienced. He was probably right but that was soon to change.

Instructions were given on expenses, reporting back,

protection of the informant, especially from Metropolitan officers and most importantly the absolute necessity not only to keep a desk diary, but also to complete daily log sheets of all activities, information and intelligence. These log sheets were to be sent by post if necessary to the Coventry office.

We left Coventry in the late morning to travel to New Scotland Yard to meet the team. We arrived in time for an afternoon conference. The main players in the forth-coming drama were all present: DI Bernard Robson, a smooth, well-spoken and somewhat superior Metropolitan officer and day-to-day Controller of Operation Coathanger; DCI Irvine, a somewhat dour Scotsman, officer in Charge of the Maidstone branch office of No6 RCS; DC Ian Bedford and WDC Jackie Everest from the same office; DS 'Dick' Barton and DC Mick Marvin from the Leicester office; and DS 'Bomber' Harris from the Brighton office. Harris was a very worldly and experienced Metropolitan officer and clearly a friend of Bernard Robson. There were other officers present, but they were to be minor players. The conference was fascinating and for me, exciting. Here I was at twenty-six a main part of a major crime investigation based at Scotland Yard.

I learned the extent of the problem and the identity of the main suspects. It was hoped that with George's help we would either catch the team in the act or, at the very least, in possession of recently stolen property.

The adventure progressed well, the team needed to gel and the main part of that was trust. The Leicester officers were sceptical of Metropolitan detectives in general, the Metropolitan officers thought we were thick and the Kent officers were wary of both.

The Coathanger squad collated details of duplicate key burglaries and liaised with the investigating officers. George needed to establish himself with the key team and Coathanger needed to trust George and his information. DI Robson stressed the need to keep our information within the squad.

Ken Brown and I made regular meetings with George and began to build a picture of who was taking part in the burglaries and who was receiving the stolen property. The main targets continued to be clothing shops. The goods were easily disposed of and not readily identifiable.

Every piece of information was logged and put into C9 and Bernard Robson. He said that we should not act too soon, for two reasons. Firstly not to 'show out' George and secondly to pull as many of the team into the frame as possible. Accordingly when George was first able to give information as to who, when and with what vehicle and also the name of a town, but not the name of the store, it was decided not to take direct action, but to pass general information to Hertfordshire who covered Hemel Hempstead where the offence was to take place. No arrests took place, but George was able to tell us what had been stolen and from where. The information was easily confirmed and greatly raised not only George's credibility but also mine and Ken's.

DI Robson's decision was proved correct, for the Coathanger team certainly gelled together. DI Robson then met George in the underground carpark at New Scotland Yard where I had taken him. DI Robson instructed George on his personal security and assured him as to the protection of his identity.

The provincial officers were billeted at Hackney section house. It was functional but no more, but our work left few idle hours so it was basically a sleeping base.

There was a great deal of satisfaction both at home and at the Yard at the progress of the operation. There was no pressure for an early result, there was only pressure from Barry Kirton to submit copies of my logs to Coventry, which I was somewhat dilatory about.

I had however become somewhat concerned about the conduct of DS Harris and told Bernard Robson that I suspected that he was 'bent'. I was told not to be concerned, officers had a difficult job in the Met and

56

methods were somewhat close to the line. Robson said he was sure that DS Harris was straight, but he was pleased that I had confided in him and that I should continue to do so. I liked Bernard and trusted him completely.

Then there came an incident which made me somewhat doubtful as to DI Robson's motives. George told me that certain members of the key team were going to enter a religious jewellery shop in Victoria Street opposite New Scotland Yard. I saw this as an ideal opportunity to arrest prominent team members 'red-handed'. Bernard did not agree. 'Small fry William, and dangerous for George. We'll wait and get them all.' I reluctantly agreed.

The burglary was carried out and George was able to pass information as to what had been stolen and where the property had been stored afterwards. The information was put into the system.

Some days later, following discussions with DCI Irvine, it was decided to carry out some early morning raids on premises occupied by and garages rented by the Lamming brothers amongst others. These were prime movers in the whole series of offences. Search warrants were obtained and the raids were to take place on the morning of Saturday 29 November 1969. The raids were to be co-ordinated by me using the team of provincial officers living at Hackney.

I was woken in the early hours of the morning by the Duty Officer at Hackney and called to the telephone.

DI Robson said, 'William, I've been stitched up. I want you to get your team up. Go out and buy enough copies of *The Times* for everyone. Read it, do not carry out the raids and all come in to the Yard at 10am.'

'What's the matter?' I asked.

Robson said, 'I've been stitched up, it's all lies, just do what I tell you.'

I roused everyone and told them to meet in the canteen. I went out to find a newsagent and bought several copies of *The Times*. I could not believe my eyes. There on the front page was a photograph of DI Robson and DS Harris apparently taking money from Michael Roy Perry, the original thief that George had identified. Even worse, inside there was a photograph of DS Symonds from Camberwell with the same man.

I returned to the section house and distributed the newspapers. I said that we should all read them before talking about it. The contents were devastating, not only were there photographs and eye witness accounts of meetings between Robson, Harris and Perry and Symonds and Perry, but the meetings had been tape recorded. It was clear that all three had been extorting money from Perry and others. It was also clear that Robson and Harris did not know about Symonds and vice versa.

The most appalling aspect of the transcripts was that they contained material that had been provided by George. The 'let's get them all William', was clearly a tactic to enable their money-making scheme to continue. DS Symonds was also clearly the source of our problem with Perry knowing the extent or lack of our evidence against him.

My head was in a whirl, and I could not believe what I was involved in. The consensus of opinion was that it must be a set-up. I was very perturbed however, by the level of detail especially in relation to the Victoria Street burglary.

We all trouped into the C9 office at New Scotland Yard at 10am. I was in a highly nervous state. I was amazed to see Robson and Harris calmly sitting at their desks writing.

I said, 'My God, you are in some bother.'

DI Robson said, 'Not at all, it's all in our diaries isn't it Bomber?'

I then saw that the two of them were writing their desk diaries, or more specifically, re-writing their desk diaries to include all the meetings covered in *The Times* articles.

'What will happen?' I asked.

Robson said, 'I'll either shake hands with the dock rail or get a new boat and call it The Good Old Times. It's a stitch-up.'

Bernard then related how he had become aware of the

article shortly after midnight and he had spent the time since then contacting various people and starting to write his desk diary.

I was more than surprised that they had not been suspended from duty and more surprised that during the morning, several well-known faces of very senior Yard personnel popped into the office and gave verbal support. One even said, 'All in your diary Bernard is it?'

'Yes, Sir,' was the reply to much laughter.

The two officers were allowed to remain on duty for three days, by which time the diaries were complete. They were then suspended.

Our enquiry was in limbo. There were long telephone conversations between me and DI Kirton at Coventry in which I told him the facts and my opinion. I also conversed with Ken James at Nuneaton. DCI Irvine took over day-to-day command of Coathanger, but it soon became clear that there were going to be problems, when the main targets were liable to be key witnesses in a corruption enquiry.

I was also able to get my first taste of what was to come when I was summoned to the office of Detective Chief Superintendent Fred Lambert, the co-head of the investigation into *The Times* allegations. I was castigated in no uncertain terms for expressing an opinion on the veracity of the allegations, this having come through a conversation with Senior RCS officers following my conversations with Barry Kirton and Ken James. I was told to keep my nose out and concentrate on the job in hand.

The 'job in hand', Coathanger, soon became untenable and I was recalled to Coventry. I also instructed George to return home.

The Times allegations were very serious because not only were there specific allegations against Robson and Harris for taking money from Perry and others to prevent their arrest, but the transcripts of the conversations between Symonds and Perry spoke of 'a firm within a firm'. Symonds was clear that no matter where in London Perry was in trouble with the police he would be able to help him, he would know someone in 'the firm' to ease the way. Symonds stressed that he had no such influence in 'the sticks' and that the 'swedes' who worked in the CID in 'the sticks' could not be bribed.

The early indication that the Metropolitan Police were not going to investigate *The Times* allegations with any urgency or thoroughness were soon dispelled. There was considerable media pressure for a thorough investigation. There was also some jockeying for position within Scotland Yard and before long both Roy York and Fred Lambert were removed from the enquiry and replaced by Detective Chief Superintendent Bill Moody. Moody had a team of young 'untouchables' as they were described. There was much trumpeting of how far-reaching the enquiry would be and that corruption would be rooted out.

The focus of the enquiry moved to Nuneaton. This was logical: Perry had become involved with Symonds through the Co-op burglary and the information Robson and Harrison had allegedly used had been supplied by an informant from the Nuneaton area, handled by me.

Moody and his team based themselves at a Nuneaton hotel and were given offices at Nuneaton police station. They made it plain before the interviews began that there would be no social contact and that the relationship was a professional one. There were many police witnesses to be interviewed, with me the prime one.

The two officers conducting my interview were a DCI Ement and DS Wally Boreham. Ement was to become Deputy Chief Constable of Thames Valley and Wally a Commander in the Met. The interview was formal, Wally was friendly, but Ement was not. I soon became uncomfortably aware that the finger was being pointed at me. I was the common denominator between all three officers and Perry. I was questioned very closely as to everything I had said and done. Written corroboration was demanded of everything I had said. Because of the need to keep logs, my desk diary contained little detail, only general references to meetings. I cited my logs as support, but was told that they did not exist; there was no trace of them at New Scotland Yard. This was hardly surprising given the amount of time between the allegations and the suspension of the officers.

At the end of the first day I was told to go home, not to leave home and not to contact any other officers. I had no wish to compromise my position, and I complied with the instructions.

The second day was more disturbing than the first. Detective Chief Superintendent Moody came into the interview room and told me that I was to be sure to tell the truth and that I was in a difficult position. When he left, I told my interviewers that there would be a copy of my logs at the Coventry office of the Regional Crime Squad. I was told later in the day that DI Kirton had refused to hand them over to a member of the enquiry team and that he had been threatened with a search warrant for the office. At the end of the second day I felt that my position was somewhat precarious. I was being treated with increasing coldness and any attempt at levity on my part was discouraged.

During the evening of that second day, I spoke to a number of people by telephone including DI Kirton. Barry told me that he was concerned that had he handed over the logs they would have been lost as the originals had been. I had also taken the opportunity to check some details relating to questions I had been asked. Barry Kirton told me that I was not to worry but to be very careful as to what I said in interview.

The interview continued on the third day until mid morning when a knock came at the interview room door. A DC from the Coventry office brought in a lever arch file containing copies of my log sheets. The DC asked me to sign for them and clearly said, 'Mr Kirton has copies of all these and you may use your copy as you wish.'

I signed and he left. Mr Ement asked to see the logs. He examined them closely and then left me with Wally

Boreham. On his return Mr Ement was a changed man. I now realise that I had changed from a potential fall guy to a major prosecution witness. I am sure that it was at this time that it was decided that Robson and Harris would have to go. The logs provided too much corroboration of *The Times* tape recordings. There was no escape for Robson, Harris and Symonds.

I made a full statement and was allowed to resume my normal duties. The duties were, however, far from normal, for although new to me were the continuing regular tasks of the Coventry office. There were also the regular contacts with George. He was also able to keep me informed of developments with the key team, their activities in both London and outside. There were however serious problems of trust. The Coathanger team was fragmented and it became increasingly obvious that the corruption in the Metropolitan CID was far reaching. The enquiry team, led by Detective Superintendent Moody was not satisfying the demands of the media, Home Office or Provincial Forces and it was decided to set up an independent investigation led by Her Majesty's Inspector of Constabulary's Assistant For Crime, Frank Williamson. The enquiry team constructed by him consisted of trusted officers from a number of forces. Frank Williamson was to be obstructed in his task to the extent that it led to his ultimate resignation.

The trial of Robson and Harris has been well documented and it is sufficient to say here that Robson was sentenced to a total of seven years and Harris six years. It was significant that just before the verdicts in their trial, and six weeks before his own trial, Symonds absconded.

There have been many theories as to why he left and I subscribed to the view that he was encouraged to depart in order to limit the investigation. It had been suggested that he was prepared to name names in his 'firm within a firm' which would have been incredibly embarrassing for the Metropolitan Police. Credence is given to this view when it is taken into account that some years later Detective Chief

Superintendent Bill Moody, who was leading *The Times* investigation was sentenced to a total of twelve years imprisonment for corruption involving very large sums of money in a trial involving what was known as 'the dirty squad'.

Symonds eventually returned to these shores from Australia and surrendered himself. He was able to arrange that his trial took place on Teeside well away from any Metropolitan influences. The memory I carry from his trial is that DS Ken James, DC Jack Wilson and I were sent back to the Midlands before giving evidence in order that Bill Moody could give his evidence, arrangements having been made to bring him from prison. We three returned the following day and were told by the Metropolitan Liaison Officer, 'Bill was here yesterday, he really did look the part.' No doubt meaning the part of a former senior officer.

But Ken James said, 'What, you mean he looked like a prisoner?'

Symonds was sentenced to a nominal term of imprisonment and in the circumstances with so much time having elapsed, justice was done.

It was agreed between Mr Williamson and the Regional Crime Squads that his team would in an emergency carry out enquiries in the Metropolitan Police district arising from Coathanger but that otherwise enquiries should concentrate in the provinces for the duration of *The Times* inquiry.

Chapter Eight

Coventry Regional Crime Squad Office

I had always been intrigued as to how the key team obtained the keys for the shops. We had learned that most shop glass doors were fitted with either Gibbons or Union locks and that the team were either using specific keys or masters from the particular suite of locks. George had been asked regularly about the suppliers of the keys but had denied all knowledge.

As our relationship progressed, it was clear that George really enjoyed his work as an informant and we decided to put him to work in Coventry. My DC, Ken Brown, had now been promoted and moved from Coventry. His replacement was a Coventry DC, Peter Whitecross, a Grade One police driver and motorcyclist, and an extremely amiable and capable detective. He and George soon established a rapport and Peter was able to point George at some local teams of villains, but hardly in the London league. We persisted in asking George about the key supplier and one day he grinned and said, 'He's in Nuneaton.'

We were amazed to learn that the man who made and supplied all the keys for all the duplicate key shop break-ins was one Charlie Robinson living in a council house in Camp Hill, Nuneaton.

Charlie had many previous convictions and had moved out of London as part of his rehabilitation. George said that Charlie not only was able to look at a shop door and identify the make of lock, but he could determine which suite of locks by watching the shop staff using the keys to open or close the doors. He could make keys from impressions and his greatest ability was to make a key by memorising the levers on a key seen hanging up or in a person's hand.

We were thrilled. DI Kirton in his usual thorough manner said that we must obtain evidence to corroborate George in order not only to protect him, but also to justify a search warrant for Robinson's house.

Surveillance of Robinson and his house was established. The former produced evidence of trips to London and meetings with known criminals and the latter evidence of visits by criminals including George! George had said that Robinson carried out his work on keys at home and it was thought that an examination of his dustbin might yield fruit. A direct approach to the house was not possible so a more subtle approach was required. We could not ask the refuse collectors to hand over the contents of a particular dustbin in case the collector told Charlie. We decided to supplement the lorry crew with one of our own staff, DC Terry Farmer, a Salvation Army trumpeter, turned detective.

Terry was put on the lorry for a week with some spurious story for the crew, the week being necessary to get the feel of the work and devise a method of retrieving the contents of Robinson's bin. The ploy was doubly successful: we recovered material from the dustbin to support our warrant and Terry changed the crew's working system, enabling the men to increase their productivity bonus.

There was now sufficient evidence to obtain a search warrant for Charlie Robinson's house and we were assured by George that there were hundreds of keys and key heads in the house.

The warrant was executed. It was a limited success. There were a number of keys, key heads, blanks and tools for key making together with a lathe. There were not 'hundreds', but there were sufficient to detain Robinson and justify the warrant.

Charlie Robinson was no help at all – he said keys were his hobby. He had been a locksmith and maintained a great interest in locks and keys. He denied all knowledge of duplicate key shop break-ins and the people involved. We questioned him for two days but it was clear that he was never going to admit anything. There was no direct evidence to connect him with burglaries and it would take much time to establish a connection between the recovered keys and specific burglaries. Charlie was bailed to re-appear at Nuneaton Police Station some weeks hence.

I saw George and told him what we had found, and he told us that we had missed most of the cache. Charlie had told him that many of the keys were concealed behind a mirror in the living room and that others were concealed in tins of food and talcum powder. Charlie was very pleased that the raid had produced what he saw as a poor result. He felt safe from prosecution.

There were two problems with undertaking a further search. We needed additional grounds to obtain another warrant and secondly we had to be very careful not to 'show out' George who was clearly closer to Charlie than we had known.

I told George of our difficulty and he suggested a solution. Charlie was not getting what he considered to be his fair share from the proceeds of the duplicate key break-ins and he had decided to carry out a burglary alone. His target was a safe in the window of a supermarket adjacent to the bus station at Nuneaton. The safe was used to hold the overnight takings and it was at that time considered to be good crime prevention practice to keep the safe in public view.

The shop glass doors were no problem to Charlie; his diffi-culty was the safe key. The safe lock was a ten lever Gibralter. Charlie, with his ability to make a key from looking at it, had taken to watching the shop manager lock the safe in the evening. The problem was that the manager held the key in such a manner that his thumb covered the tenth lever. George said that Charlie felt that he had the first nine levers, but could not cut the tenth. He had entered the shop on several occasions, but was obviously limited as to how much time he could spend in the window. George told us that Charlie was at the supermarket from 5.30–6pm most weekdays.

Barry Kirton decided that he and I, who both lived in Nuneaton, would watch the supermarket each evening on our way home and that we would be able to judge when Charlie had achieved his objective. We hoped to catch him entering the shop which would also justify a further search of his home.

A good observation point was essential. We did not want to involve the supermarket manager and approached the friend of a policeman's widow who managed a television rental shop nearby. She readily gave us a key and access to a first floor room. Barry and I began our daily vigil. Sure enough Charlie turned up on the first day and watched the manager lock the safe. He then left. I had already arranged for George to let me know if he heard anything from Charlie and we decided that Charlie's conduct was insufficient to justify arrest.

Barry and I continued to watch Charlie for a number of days, but there was no change in his demeanour. He clearly could not get a view of the whole key. One particular day Barry, having become somewhat frustrated, said, 'Come on let's nick him. We've got enough.'

We left the TV shop and crossed the road towards Charlie. He immediately saw us and recognising us, he began to shout, 'It ain't fair, it ain't fair, the police are coming for me, it ain't fair.'

He could see that we were not diverted by his shouting and when we took hold of him he struggled violently. We held him and frog-marched him to the police station. We dared not search him as it would have necessitated letting go of his arms. In the charge room at the police station we let his arms go, preparatory to searching him. He immediately put his hand in his pocket and then put his hand to his mouth and started chewing. We took hold of him and he struggled violently. We got him to the ground, forced his mouth open, and I put my fingers inside and withdrew a screwed up piece of paper. We were unable to read it at this time, as he was still struggling. We subdued him and having completed our search, examined the piece of paper. There was a London telephone number written on it. Charlie was asked what the number referred to and why he had tried to swallow it. He did not answer.

There was some urgency in the situation, but as we could not trust some elements of the Metropolitan Police CID at this time, Barry decided to ring the Williamson team at Tintagel House where they were based. He related our story and they promised to act on it.

Barry was anxious to search Charlie's house before it became known that he was in custody. He summoned officers from our Coventry office and we all went to Camp Hill, including Charlie.

Great restraint was needed to not immediately rush to the mirror. A systematic search took place which revealed keys inside two tins of talcum powder and strangely a number of tins of kipper fillets in the airing cupboard. It was decided to remove the kipper tins for further examination.

Eventually, the mirror was examined, but there was no obvious place of concealment. Charlie was asked whether there was anything behind the mirror. He said there was not. George had said that there was a button release to the mechanism. A number of screws were pressed and sure enough, up came the back of the mirror which consisted of a number of shelves, each carrying a few tobacco tins. Each tin was lined with cotton wool, and in each there were a number of key heads which turned out to be glass door keys. We were elated, Charlie was not. He refused any explanation and we all returned to Nuneaton police station.

The kipper fillet tins were examined and were found to have been opened and resealed. Each one contained a number of Gibbons master key heads, Gibbons being the main manufacturer of locks for glass doors.

We had clearly struck gold and this was confirmed when later that evening *The Times* enquiry team rang to say that the address relating to the telephone number had been searched and contained many thousands of pounds' worth of clothing stolen the previous evening by duplicate key from a shop in the Home Counties. The flat was occupied by two men well known from the Coathanger enquiry.

Charlie Robinson had a lot of explaining to do and eventually decided to offer limited co-operation. He took great care not to implicate others but admitted some part in the whole conspiracy. This partial confession could not be relied on and it was necessary to conduct an extensive enquiry into the origin and purpose of the recovered keys. This necessitated many weeks of leg-work visiting lock and safe manufacturers throughout England. It was a very interesting exercise and also produced more than sufficient evidence to convict Charlie Robinson. Charlie received a lengthy prison sentence and because of his unique talents he was a security risk, serving much of his sentence at HMP Gartree, Leicestershire.

It is widely believed that it was not a coincidence that very shortly after Charlie's release, there was a mass breakout from Gartree using duplicate keys made from plastic toothbrush handles!

The Coventry office of the number 4 RCS was only a small one. There were five two-man crews, a DI and DCI with one female admin support staff. The tasks were varied across the whole criminal calendar. Some tasks were self-generated and others nominated by the local forces. There were also requirements to supplement the enquiry teams on major incidents such as murder. We were treated as something of an elite on such occasions and were always given 'live' enquiries relating to suspects.

69

George became a valuable asset during my two-year secondment. Not only was he to be the author of the downfall of a number of Coventry criminals but he was also still able to provide accurate and timely intelligence on crime and criminals in both the Metropolitan police district and the City of London. We found that we were able to liaise successfully with other RSC officers from both number 9 and number 1 Crime Squads. George had an amazing ability to involve himself with the most established teams of criminals, often enabling them to be caught in the act and always providing the best intelligence of principles and associates. There were always concerns as to his safety and more particularly his honesty and his own criminal activities. We were not foolish enough to think that George was able to infiltrate these teams of criminals without proving his worth. We constantly impressed upon him his need for caution in all these areas.

Colleagues in the city of London became concerned that George was associating with a team who were known to deal in forged bank notes, but was not producing information as to their distribution. We were aware that forged £5 notes were circulating in the Coventry area and were fearful that George was 'importing' them when we brought him back from London after his forays in the city. I had no wish to sour our relationship by directly accusing him or searching him before driving him home. Our relationship was based on a considerable element of trust. It was arranged that city officers would stop George as he arrived at our pre-arranged rendezvous and search him. He was clean.

We continued to be wary but thought no more of the forged £5 notes until one weekday morning we read on the local crime sheet that George's wife had been caught passing a forged £5 note in Marks & Spencer's in Coventry the previous Saturday. No action had been taken as she was considered to be an innocent party!

I was furious. Peter and I had no difficulty in obtaining a

search warrant for George's house. I knew that if we were to take action against him, it would have to be 'by the book'.

Peter and I turned up at George's house with the warrant. George had clearly seen us arrive and greeted us in his usual affable manner. This changed when I produced the warrant – he was very shaken and obviously worried. He denied all knowledge of forged notes and invited me to search the house. We began a systematic search of the house and garden, keeping George with us, but allowing his wife to carry on looking after the children. As the search progressed George became cockier and cockier – it was like a game of hide and seek, and we were getting colder and colder. We were convinced that we were right and that there were forged £5 notes in the house, but we could not find them and eventually had to leave.

The incident did not affect our relationship with George although his usefulness declined due to him becoming too well known. There were only so many times that he could be used without exposure. There were also one or two cases where there was more than a hint of 'agent provocateur'. I think he was beginning to enjoy it too much.

It was some months after the search of his house that I asked George where the forged fivers had been hidden. He laughed and said, 'They were in a plastic bag going round with the washing in the washing machine.'

I never forgot that lesson and always ensured that active washing machines were switched off and drained during future raids, especially when I became involved with the Drug Squad.

There was one particularly memorable enquiry during my secondment to the crime squad when we became involved with a team we came to call 'The Quality Street Gang'. It was at this time that Quality Street were advertised by a bunch of ill-assorted cartoon characters of gangster appearance. They were somewhat inept, unlike their namesakes.

They came to our attention through a complaint from a hitherto law-abiding businessman who ran two supermarkets in the Coventry suburbs. The businessman had been approached by two Londoners. Having engaged him in conversation and ascertained his business, they sold him two Rolex wrist watches at what was clearly a knock-down price and intimated that they were stolen property. Within a week or so contact was re-established and an offer of a van load of cigarettes for several thousand pounds was made. The price was a fraction of the true value and the shopkeeper bit. He arranged to raise the cash with his uncle and complicated arrangements were made for the handover, resulting in one of the sellers staying with the money and the second going off to the van, each with one of the two businessmen. The Londoners, by an obviously well practised routine, managed to lose their companions but retained the money and, of course, there were no cigarettes.

It was a very clever scam – they had ensured the dishonesty of the victim by selling him the watches, then waited a decent interval to see whether he had reported to the police that he had bought stolen property. Highly unlikely. They had then made him an offer that was too good to refuse. Greed was the key. The offenders also knew that it would be very rare for anyone to go to the police and say, 'I was trying to buy some stolen property, but it was a con.'

However, on this occasion, they came unstuck.

Their main downfall was that the local CID passed the enquiry to the RCS office where Barry Kirton took charge. To describe Barry as a terrier would be an understatement; a wolf-hound would be more accurate. He would never give up the chase and when caught the quarry would not escape.

Enquiries were made of Regional Crime Intelligence Offices, for it was obvious that the Coventry case was not a one-off. A number of similar offences were discovered, in Warwickshire and surrounding counties. It was clear that this team had been working for some years and were very successful. There was no way of ever knowing the ratio of reported to unreported offences, but it must have been at least one-to-five and probably one-to-ten.

We collated details of the offences, descriptions of the offenders, details of their MO, names, places talked of, vehicles used and gradually built up a picture of 'The Quality Street Gang'.

The method was always the same and their main targets were metal dealers. The team would frequent pubs where metal dealers were known to gather. They would select the target and go into the Rolex watch routine. In the unfortunate rare event of being reported to the police as being in possession of stolen watches, which did happen, the men were able to produce genuine receipts for the watches. The receipts showed that they were selling at a great loss, this they explained as a 'come-on' to get the confidence of the dealers to do business with them – they would recover their loss in future dealings.

Invariably of course, there were no reports to the police and the scam continued. With metal dealers it was always a lorry-load of stolen copper. With shopkeepers, it was cigarettes or confectionery.

The descriptions and MO were sufficient for DI Kirton to identify a number of London men, in particular two brothers, one of whom bore more than a passing resemblance to Alistair Sim, a description given in the Coventry case and others.

The men lived in the area covered by the Barkingside office of the Regional Crime Squad, run by a DI Polkinghorn. It was agreed that on a specific day Barkingside would arrest as many of the team as possible and we would escort them to Coventry to be interviewed.

The early morning visits were in the main successful and all the major players, apart from the elder brother 'Charlie', were arrested.

They were escorted back to Coventry and interviewed at length. They were not at all helpful. Barry Kirton decided to hold a series of identity parades at Coventry utilising a large number of witnesses from various parts of the Midlands. I was highly optimistic of a full identification of 'Alistair Sim' by our two Coventry complainants. I was wrong; they failed to pick him out. I never knew why, but I suspect it was fear of repercussions.

There were a number of successful identifications, particularly by two metal dealers from Sheffield who had lost £3,000. The offenders were all bailed for further enquiries to be made.

One of the enquiries concerned 'Charlie'. It was found that his file, under his correct name, had been drawn nineteen times in two years from CRO, but he had never been charged. No-one can be that lucky. We suspected that we were up against our old friend 'corruption'. Our suspicions were strengthened when our repeated requests to Barkingside for Charlie's arrest were met with 'He wasn't in guv', or, 'He's gone away.'

Barry Kirton told DI Polkinghorn that if there was no result the following day, Pete Whitecross and I would be sent down and stay until we had found Charlie.

Surprise, surprise, the following day he was in. Pete and I were despatched to escort him to Coventry.

Charlie was a most engaging character, and we had an extremely entertaining journey back to Coventry. Charlie refused to talk about the current enquiry, but regaled us with stories about his early criminal career and his dealings with villains and policemen. He made it plain that 'in the past' he had paid large sums of money to ensure his continued freedom. Pete and I took this with a pinch of salt, but we soon discovered that he had managed to glean a lot of personal information about Pete, Barry and I from us and his associates.

At Coventry he was interviewed at length by Barry Kirton. He denied all knowledge of the offences and knowledge of his brother's activities. Identity parades were set up and he was picked out by all the witnesses we had selected, but he still refused to admit any part in the scam.

74

It was decided to bail Charlie for a few weeks in order to strengthen our case. On being bailed he was told that he would have to make his own way home and that there was a train to London in an hour and a half. He asked for a lift to the railway station, Barry agreed and we all three took him there. It was early evening and Charlie proposed that we all took a meal in the Chinese restaurant opposite the Railway station. Barry agreed with the proviso that we all paid for our own meals. We all sat down to a very convivial meal.

Part way through the meal Charlie said, 'Barry, they tell me you are buying your own house.' County Officers had formerly been obliged to live in police houses until our amalgamation with Coventry city. Barry confirmed this and Charlie said, 'How much are houses round here Barry?'

Barry said, 'I'm buying a detached house in Nuneaton for £6,750.'

Charlie said, 'I tell you what Barry. The others will plead guilty. I'll buy the house for you and give Bill and Pete three grand each if you let me out.'

Barry was apoplectic, he was spitting rice all over the table and said, 'You are going down, you can't buy your way out of things up here, you've made a serious mistake.'

He got up and ordered Pete and I to leave with him.

All the team were committed to Warwick for trial and all but Charlie pleaded guilty. Charlie was found guilty by the jury and sentenced to two years' imprisonment.

Barry took great delight in going down to the cells and saying, 'I told you that you can't buy your way out in the country!'

Secondment to the RCS was for no more than two years and it was unusual for this to be extended. It became important to find yourself a job before the end of your time. It was not unknown for officers to have to undergo a spell in uniform before finding a position in the CID. The obvious way was to discover the identity of your replacement and endeavour to arrange a straight swop. My replacement was to be Ken Cook, a Coventry DS based at Willenhall, an independent section on the south west of the city. The position was an interesting one in that it was based in a police 'box' in the shopping precinct of a large council estate. The DS had responsibility for two DCs and some supervisory role of a dozen Constables working under a uniformed Sergeant. I was successful in arranging the swop and so began an interesting two years.

Chapter Nine

Willenhall

I have often said that I dealt with every offence in the criminal calendar at Willenhall – certainly most of them occurred and the CID element dealt with the majority. The uniform staff were first class, keen and industrious, led by a very dynamic Sergeant. The level of intelligence was excellent, due not only to the application of the staff, but also to the fact that there was continuity of staffing with some both working and living on the section.

There were a number of hardened criminals living on this section, some of them forming criminal families. There was extreme poverty, regular domestic violence, and many burglaries and thefts. There was a strong element of anti-police feeling, but also elements of support. On a number of occasions the 'box' was besieged when a prominent criminal was held for interview or in custody pending transfer to Little Park Street police station in the City Centre. On one memorable occasion, I and one of my DCs were unable to leave the 'Winnall' pub until a uniform escort arrived due to one family waiting to attack us outside the pub. They could not carry out the assault inside for fear of being barred, this fear being greater than that of a fine or imprisonment.

The council estate contained one of the largest working men's clubs in the Midlands. It was so large that there were two stewards, one for the 'top' and one for the 'bottom'. It was an extremely active club holding regular dances, concerts, bingo and a tote. This was in addition to a number of bars, gaming machines and snooker tables. The turnover was very large and the club was managed by a committee of twenty-two members. It had long been a joke that the first prize in the raffle was 'a fortnight on the committee'. It was to our knowledge very well run: there was very little trouble, inside or outside the club, for the committee were very quick to suspend any member committing a nuisance or misbehaving in any way.

Then we received a report that a committee member had been caught fiddling the tote. The treasurer, an unemployed postman, reported that the member had been caught writing in the winning numbers against his name after he had been present at the Sunday morning draw of the tote numbers. It was most unusual for such a crime to be reported and I was intrigued.

An interview was arranged with the treasurer who was most anxious to provide evidence against the individual concerned. Some pressure had clearly been applied by club members for the matter to be reported. The Treasurer's position was an elected one and although only paid an honorarium, he was keen to retain what was an important social position.

I insisted on taking the tote books for the previous two years in order to see the extent of the 'offender's' wins before interviewing him.

Examination of the books was most revealing: firstly the 'offender' had won on a number of occasions and secondly there was never a single winner – the prize was always shared. It was a cash prize and a substantial sum, as the tote was very well supported. I could see that there were a number of names that regularly appeared as winners, including the treasurer.

I obtained a list of names of the committee. The first startling fact was that of the twenty-two, only two were employed. The second was that eight of them regularly won the tote. I made further enquiries and found that all commit-tee men had specific tasks involving the handling of cash. In addition to supervising the tote, there was the bingo, the door of the dance where cash was collected for admission, and the emptying of the gaming machines. The stewards did not allow any interference whatsoever behind the bar other than by employed staff. It began to appear that 'a fortnight on the committee' was a prize worth winning!

We arrested the original suspect and interviewed him at the 'box' in the precinct. He was, as usual, reluctant to admit his part, but eventually admitted the one offence for which he had been reported. There was no doubt that he was lying, but he was extremely worried about implicating others. I released him after obtaining samples of his signa-ture and handwriting.

Some days later, I received a telephone call from a man who asked to meet me away from Willenhall. I arranged to meet him on the other side of the city. The man was a committee member and wanted to 'blow the whistle' on the fiddles at the social club. He told me that the tote fiddle had been going on for years and in order that it did not become too obvious that the committee who drew the tote were winning on a regular basis, they were using assumed names and signing in those names. He also revealed that the bingo takings were systematically plundered and the same was true of the dance takings and gaming machine proceeds. He declined to detail his own part but he said that it was time to get it stopped as it was now completely out of hand.

It was immediately clear that this wholesale fraud would be extremely difficult to prove. I intended to prove as much as possible and then let it be known at the club the extent of what we believed to be the scale of theft. I obtained signa-ture and handwriting samples from all the committee and left them all into no doubt as to what we thought and that we intended to prove as much as possible.

The signature and handwriting samples showed me that the same hands had written many of the winners' signatures.

I knew from experience that my perception would not necessarily be backed up by the handwriting experts at the forensic science laboratory. To secure a conviction we would need them to say that the writing was identical. I took their advice that they would never be able to say any more than that there were striking similarities. I would therefore need some corroborative evidence such as a confession or a statement of implication. Neither was likely as feelings at the club were running very high and an admission by anyone would not only lead to a conviction and expulsion but almost certainly a beating.

We arrested a number of the committee, but no admissions were forthcoming. Evidence was sufficient to prosecute only a handful and these pleaded guilty and were fined. Many of the committee were not re-elected and I am sure that the club revenue increased dramatically.

A side benefit was that I and my DCs were always welcome in the club and well looked after.

The beauty of community policing, that is where the police are based in the community they serve, is that the police pick up gossip and rumour as well as concrete information and intelligence. It reached our ears that a local girl had given birth to a child and that the body had been burned in the back garden of her house. The rumour grew in strength as the day progressed and it was clear there was a lot of bad feeling on the estate, as it was suggested that the baby had been born alive. This put the matter into an entirely different category – it was a potential murder.

The family concerned was well known to us and the alleged mother was the eldest daughter of the house. I made some preliminary enquiries and confirmed that the girl had been pregnant and was recently in the advanced stages. I conferred with my DCI at Little Park Street, Alf Horrobin, an aggressive import to the West Midlands. He told me to go to the house and 'play it by ear'.

It was dark by the time that this stage had been reached. I went to the house with a DC and uniform assistance. I told the mother of the family what I wanted and both she and her daughter denied that a birth had taken place. The daughter did not look well and was clearly very concerned. I made a preliminary search of the house and found some blood-stained bedding. The explanation given for this was 'heavy periods'.

A search turned to the 'garden', an area of wasteland. We had torches and found a dustbin in the middle of the garden in which there had been a fire. Examination of the contents by torch-light revealed nothing of interest. There were no signs of a fire elsewhere in the garden or house and I decided to remove the dustbin to the police 'box'. I left a uniformed presence at the house with instructions not to allow anyone to leave without my permission.

I took the dustbin back to the 'box' and placed it on the floor in the kitchen. I could see that the bin was three-quarters full with burned material. I carefully poked about in the bin and at the bottom found some blankets which were partly burned and fused together. I gently prized them apart and inside was a perfect new born baby, dead but apparently untouched by the fire. I did not examine the body further but left to telephone DCI Horrobin.

He said, 'Don't move. Wait there. I'm coming up.'

The DCI arrived within ten or fifteen minutes. He stormed into my office and shouted. 'Have you taken leave of your senses Sergeant? Moving a body from a murder scene. Don't you know anything? I'll have you out for this. You are finished. Where is it?'

I said, 'In the kitchen sir.'

He stormed out and returned within a minute and said, 'Where in the kitchen?'

'In the dustbin,' I replied.

Off he went again, only to return shortly afterwards demanding, 'Where in the dustbin? Show me.'

I followed him into the kitchen and showed him the baby inside the fused blankets. Before he could speak, I said, 'You expected me to see it in the dark outside, when you can't see it inside in the light.'

The DCI said, 'All right, point taken, but you should not have moved it.'

I did not argue, as past experience had told me that it was pointless. I merely said, 'Am I to carry on or are you doing it?'

The DCI said, 'Carry on, but keep me informed.'

I 'carried on', removal was authorised to the mortuary and the suspected mother was arrested and interviewed. The house was closely examined and a number of items removed.

The interview with the girl was very carefully undertaken; she was in a poor emotional and physical state and was not very bright. She admitted giving birth, but said she was alone and that the child was born dead. She was frightened and decided to burn the dead body to prevent anyone knowing about the baby. I did not believe that she had acted alone especially with such a large family in a small house. I saw little point in interviewing other members of the family until we had the results of the post-mortem. There were a number of possible charges: murder, manslaughter, infanticide, child destruction and concealment of birth. There was no danger of further offences and after taking advice I bailed the girl, who was in her late teens, to re-appear at the police station following the post-mortem.

The Willenhall population and the police, including myself, were convinced that the child had been born alive and killed by preventing breathing. The only opinion that mattered was that of the pathologist.

I attended the post-mortem at Coventry and Warwickshire Hospital. I knew that in the absence of any injuries, the key was whether the child had taken a breath. My very limited medical knowledge was such that I knew that if the lungs floated when put into water, then there was air in them and a breath had been taken.

The pathologist and I had conversed during his examination of the poor little soul and he was well aware of my view. The time came for the little lungs to be removed and placed in the jar – they floated.

'Born alive,' I said.

'Born dead Sergeant.'

'Oh come on Doc,' I said.

'Tell me what good it will do, if I say born alive?' said the doctor.

He was right of course.

I charged the girl with concealment of birth and she was placed under supervision. No other member of the family was taken to court but I am sure that justice was done.

One case at Willenhall changed my entire view of the strength of a very important aspect of evidence in criminal cases.

Mother's Pride Bakery had a depot on an industrial estate at Tollbar. We received a call that a roundsman had absconded with his week's takings of several hundred pounds in cash. A visit to the depot revealed that the roundsman had only been employed for a few weeks and his references had yet to be returned. Urgent enquiries of the referees by the bakery, following his disappearance, had shown them to be totally false, as were his name, address and national insurance number.

There were many people who had seen the man on a daily basis and we were able to put together a very good physical description, together with details of who, what, and where he had spoken of in conversation. He had regularly spoken of Falkirk in Scotland and as we were getting nowhere with other enquiries, I rang Falkirk police. The officer with whom I spoke gave me the name of a man who fitted the description and had previous convictions for theft. The officer told me that he would send me a photograph of this man.

The rules on photographic identification were strict and apart from using a minimum number of photographs, it was essential to retain some witnesses for a possible future identification parade who had not been shown photographs.

I selected three members of staff who had seen the man

regularly, showed the photographs independently and all three picked out the suspect without hesitation. Bingo!

I circulated the details of the man as wanted for theft of cash whilst employed as a baker's roundsman and awaited results.

Some weeks later, I received a telephone call from the CID in Leeds to say that they had my man in custody. He had been arrested for other matters and a check with CRO had revealed that he was wanted. I told Leeds to keep him and I would travel up to collect him.

I travelled to Leeds with another officer and brought my prisoner back to Coventry. He was no trouble but denied the offence absolutely and also said that he had never visited Coventry in his life. He persisted with his story in a formal interview, but I was not perturbed by his attitude as it was not unusual. I had plenty of witnesses and decided to run an identification parade.

The parade was run by a uniformed Inspector; I had no part in it other than to select the witnesses and silently observe the proceedings. I selected five witnesses, two of whom had seen photographs. The parade members were selected from the street. They were of similar appearance and the prisoner did not object to any of them.

All five witnesses picked him out without hesitation. He moved his position between parades, but to no avail. He was 'bang to rights'.

I conducted a further interview following the parades. He continued to deny the offence and maintained his assertion that he had never visited Coventry previously. I played the whole thing absolutely to the book; no 'gilding of lilies'. In due course, the man was committed for trial at the Crown Court. I was fully confident of a conviction.

Two weeks after the committal, I received a telephone call from Kennington Oval Police Station in London.

'Hello guv,' said a Met officer. 'We've got a guy here admitting stealing some money from a bakery in Coventry.'

I said, 'No, we've got him, he must be having you on.'

The Met officer was able to give me details of dates and amounts together with the details of the bread round the man was allocated to. I could not believe it: I told the Met to hold on to the man and, with a colleague, I drove to London.

I questioned the man and was soon convinced that he was the Mother's Pride rounds-man and it was not my man from Leeds. What a mess! The London man did not look in any way like the other. The second man was taller and thinner, and had different coloured hair and different shaped features. I was thankful that the original prisoner had been granted bail having shown a settled address and provided sureties.

Proceedings were discontinued against the first man and the second man pleaded guilty.

I saw all the witnesses again, but they remained convinced that they had picked out the right man!

I was very wary thereafter on uncorroborated witness identification, even five fold!

Chapter Ten

Policemen and Guns!

I had during my time on the regional crime squad, become a very proficient shot with a Browning 9mm pistol due to the encouragement of my DC, Peter Whitecross, who was a former sniper and natural shot, coupled with the opportunity to practise once or twice a week at the Gamecock barracks of the Junior Leaders Regiment at Nuneaton. Firearms use in Warwickshire and Coventry was in its infancy when I was doing this and I was soon selected as a member of the Force Firearms Team. The officer in charge, Ian McCardle, took over the responsibility for the Force Firearms Team of the West Midlands Police when it was formed in 1974. I remained a member of the team from its inception in Warwickshire in 1970 through to 1982. During this long period, I was required to be armed on many occasions, but it was very rare indeed for the firearm to be drawn with intent to fire. Most incidents were protective, either as prisoner or VIP escort. I had attended a two-week VIP protection firearms course in Devon and Cornwall concerned solely with threat potential and reaction in VIP protection situations. I required this for Special Branch duties from 1979 to 1981. There were three events relating to firearms that are worth recalling: two with comic outcomes and one with far-reaching consequences in many areas.

The first arose from firearms training. Training took

place at Kinsgbury firearms range where outdoor scenarios were enacted, and at an old city centre police station for urban sequences. All the training days included a qualification shoot to maintain standards. The intensity and realism of the training increased as the criminal use of firearms became more widespread. Wax bullets were used to teach you 'to keep your head down'. If hit by such a missile it hurt both your body and your pride.

At one practice I was teamed with a DC, Geoff, a Special Branch Officer at Coventry with whom I had become friendly. I was at the time a Detective Sergeant at Fletchamstead police station in Coventry.

Geoff and I had to cross open ground to reach a building where the 'criminal' was holed-up. I sent Geoffrey across at a run while I covered him. Geoffrey ran and threw himself down behind cover and as he did so, I heard a loud crack. He had broken his leg! The exercise was halted and we ran to where he lay. First aid was administered; he was told not to move and given a cigarette! Geoff was in great pain, but all he could say was, 'My holidays. My holidays, I'm going to Cornwall in a fortnight, I won't be able to drive.'

I said, 'Don't worry about it. We'll sort it out. Just keep still.'

'My wife can't drive,' continued Geoff. 'We won't be able to go.'

'If you can't get anyone,' I assured him, 'I'll take you, don't worry.'

An ambulance arrived and he was taken to hospital.

Two weeks later, I found myself driving Geoff, his wife and daughter Natalie to Newquay in Cornwall – a distance of three hundred miles, one way! I drove overnight on Friday and returned on the Saturday morning. I then had to repeat the six hundred mile journey a fortnight later. Traffic in the 1970s was a nightmare and I told myself to keep my mouth shut in the future. I did not learn from the experience however.

87

Some years later when I was a DCI in charge of the Force Drug Squad, and Geoffrey was still in the Special Branch at Coventry where I had been their DI for a time in the intervening years, I received a telephone call from him.

'Gaffa,' he said, 'you know I'm in some bother?'

I confirmed that I did. Geoff had been arrested for drink driving whilst on duty. He had been involved in an accident one evening and failed a breath test. Geoff continued and said, 'I need some advice. I've been to court, I was fined and disqualified, but now I have got to appear before the Chief. What should I do?'

I advised Geoff that there were only two courses of action that the Chief Constable, Sir Philip Knights, could take under the disciplinary regulations. One was to reprimand him and the other was to dismiss Geoff from the force. I said that Geoff should plead guilty and get someone to mitigate on his behalf.

Geoff asked, 'Who shall I get?'

I said, 'You want someone personable, confident, a good speaker and not afraid of appearing in front of the Chief.'

'So what are you doing that day?'

I had opened my mouth again!

The day of the hearing was when I was on holiday in Devon with my family. I had to travel back for the day to represent Geoff at the hearing. My wife was delighted!

I had discussed the mitigation with Geoffrey and had decided to play on the fact that he had consumed the drink which caused his downfall at the house of an Asian contact whom he was trying to recruit as an informant. I would also emphasise that Geoffrey had collided with a parked and unattended vehicle. I added that I would modify this dependent upon what the presenting officer said. I knew that the Chief Constable was supposed to be ignorant of the facts other than those presented to him.

The hearing was in the afternoon which allowed me to make the journey in the morning and return in the evening.

The facts were presented and were really quite bald: an

accident, no injuries, no other driver, over the limit, convicted at magistrates' court, fined and disqualified. Quite straightforward. No previous disciplinary matters. Simple, I thought.

'You are aware Sir,' I began, 'that my friend is a Special Branch Officer of many years' experience and that on the evening in question, he had spent some time at the house of an Asian contact whom he was hoping to recruit as an informant on extremist matters.'

I looked at the Chief, but he showed no reaction, just looked straight at me.

I continued, 'You are also aware that Asians are particularly hospitable and that they had for this special occasion prepared food and drink. The drink offered was barcardi and coke.' I looked at the Chief. 'A white rum sir, from the Caribbean.'

No reaction.

'My friend accepted the drink in order not to offend, and during the evening he had two of these drinks. It was a drink he was unused to and the measures may have been large. He left the house in his car. It was a strange area to him, a new housing estate. The drink had perhaps affected him somewhat, the area was poorly lit and he collided with a parked, unlit and unattended motorcar.'

'Where was it parked Mr Hannis?' said the Chief.

He's read the file, I thought. Oh dear. 'The car was parked, unlit and unattended outside the owner's house sir.'

'Where exactly, Mr Hannis?'

Oh yes, he's read the file, I thought.

'The car was parked unlit and unattended outside the owners' garage sir.'

'Where is the garage Mr Hannis?' said the Chief with a weary air.

'At the bottom of the drive sir.'

'Yes Mr Hannis and your friend travelled through two gardens to get there, did he not?'

'Yes, sir,' I said.

'It must have been very strong white rum from the Caribbean Mr Hannis.'

I nodded and smiled weakly.

Character evidence was given by the Special Branch Superintendent and then the Chief Constable pronounced to the court his decision, saying, 'I am sure that your learned friend, Mr Hannis, has explained that I can either reprimand you or require you to resign from the force. On this occasion, I will reprimand you.'

I am sure that Sir Philip had made his decision before my eloquent appeal, fortunately! Geoffrey was very relieved and I readily accepted his thanks for saving him from the sack.

The second firearms incident was also during my time at Fletchamstead Police station. Firearms training had developed to where in addition to using handguns and sniper rifles, we had taken into use a shotgun which was multipurpose. It was designed to use three types of ammunition: 00 buckshot – stopping power without, hopefully, fatal injury; a Ferret gas cartridge to introduce tear gas into buildings or vehicles; and a rifled lead slug which was intended for stopping vehicles by smashing the engine block. We had practised with it and it was accurate over short distances. It had yet to be used in anger.

I was Duty DS at 'M3' as the Fletchamstead sub division was now known in the West Midlands Police. It was Boxing Day of 1974. The Owners of Whitley Zoo had reported the escape of a wild boar from its compound. The escapee was a fully grown and fully tusked animal which was considered extremely dangerous. It was a quiet day and I wandered along out of interest. A search had been organised by the Chipperfields who were the owners of the zoo. They were concerned that the animal would attack anyone surprising it and it was capable of inflicting fatal injuries by ripping open the femoral artery with its tusks. Mr Chipperfield said that the animal should be shot, but it would take a substantial weapon to halt it. I immediately thought of the rifled slug intended for stopping cars. It was by now dusk and the search was to be called off for the night. I obtained written authority to draw a shotgun and ammunition from Acocks Green police station the following morning.

I collected the gun and then reported to the zoo. I was to remain on standby at the zoo until the animal was sighted. I was then to attend the location and shoot the boar. Simple!

I was to be accompanied on my hunt by Mr Chipperfield and as I waited with him, he entertained me with lurid tales of injuries inflicted by maddened boars. He said that I should aim just behind the shoulder to be sure of stopping the boar and preventing it carrying through its attack. I began to think that I had opened my mouth at the wrong time again! I was becoming more and more apprehensive about my role as a 'big white hunter'.

Before too long a call came to say that the boar had been sighted. We had just become mobile when another call informed us that the boar had run on to the main Coventry to London railway line and had been hit and killed by a train. I was rather relieved and soon recovered myself enough to pose for a photograph with the dead boar back at the zoo.

The third incident related to the Birmingham Pub Bombings on 22 November 1974.

I had finished duty at Coventry on what was the day of Patrick McDade's funeral. He was an IRA terrorist who had blown himself up planting a bomb in Coventry. It had been a difficult day and had passed off, as we thought, peacefully. I was having a drink in the bar of the fire station across the road from Fletchamstead police station when I was recalled. I was told that a bomb had exploded in Birmingham city centre and that several people had been killed. The Assistant Chief Constable (Crime) Harry Robinson was running the enquiry and had asked for assistance from Divisions of any Detectives who could be spared. I volunteered to go with WDC Carol Clarke. We were told not to go to the scene but to report to Police Headquarters at Lloyd House.

I drove quickly to Birmingham where Carol and I joined many other Detectives. There appeared to be no organisation and much rumour flying about. There was a call for silence and all firearms trained officers were told to report to a particular room. I reported to a DCI in the room and was issued with a handgun and ammunition. I was allocated to another DCI in charge of a team of a dozen detectives. There was certainty that the IRA was responsible for the bombings and there was confirmation that many people had been killed and injured. Feeling was running high and clearly intelligence was poor. The Special Branch had provided names and addresses of a number of potential suspects and these had been divided amongst the operational teams. My team had been allocated three addresses. The DCI announced that we would all travel together and hit each address in turn. I asked who else was armed apart from myself and the DCI said, 'Just you son. There's only one to each team.'

We arrived at the first address and the DCI said, 'Right son, in you go and tell me when it's clear.'

'What, on my own?'

'You've got the gun,' he said. 'You clear the house.'

I knocked loudly and when the door was answered, I shouted, 'Police!' I pushed the man out of the way and went through the house, putting all the lights on and shouting, 'Police! Stay where you are.'

I was followed by the others who questioned the occupants and looked around the house. I had been in something of a nervous state throughout.

I could not see the sense in pussyfooting around and told the DCI so.

He said, 'Do it how you like at the next one.'

The second address was said to be occupied by active IRA sympathisers. We arrived there and I put the front door in, went in gun in hand, kicking doors and shouting, 'Armed police, stay where you are.'

The house was occupied by a large family with children. I succeeded in badly frightening them all. The intelligence was clearly inaccurate and out of date. The DCI decided to 'softly, softly' at the third address, and again it was a negative visit.

We returned weary and somewhat dispirited to Headquarters where we were buoyed up by finding that a number of men had been arrested on the Holyhead train. They were Irish and travelling from Birmingham. Senior officers said that they were clearly involved. It was by this time after six in the morning as we were released to return to our home stations.

I found Carol and we set off along the M6 for Coventry. We had not travelled far when the car began to overheat badly. I pulled on to the hard shoulder and on lifting the bonnet saw that the fan belt had broken. I had no wish to extend my tour of duty any longer and although being no mechanic, I knew that ladies' tights made a good emergency fan belt.

'Carol,' I said, 'get your tights off.'

'You must be joking,' she replied.

'It's that or we wait for the police garage,' I told her.

'Turn round then,' she said.

I soon had a new fan-belt fitted and we were eating a full breakfast at Fletchamstead within half an hour.

Chapter Eleven

Fletchamstead and Promotion to Inspector

My time at Willenhall was coming to a close. The section was under the supervision of Little Park Street Police station, and I assumed that I would be transferred there. I had undertaken a number of night duty shifts at that station and was familiar with the staff. Boundary changes were in the offing as was a further amalgamation. Coventry and Warwickshire was being split. Coventry, Solihull and Sutton Coldfield were to be part of the new West Midlands Force and the remainder of Warwickshire was to be an autonomous constabulary, the second smallest in England. I was transferred to Fletchamstead Highway Police station. Willenhall was to be part of that sub-division in the West Midlands Police. As a DS at 'M3' as it was known, I was responsible for a shift of three DCs, all of them Scotsmen. The work was very varied: there were good class housing areas and very poor council estates, major industrial sites such as Triumph motorcars and small industrial units. There were thefts, wounding, arson, sexual offences and frauds enough to keep the CID fully occupied.

The amalgamation was a serious dilemma for many officers, including myself. As a former County Officer, I had the choice between the two forces. West Midlands was an unknown quantity and an amalgamation of parts of Warwickshire, Birmingham, Wolverhampton, Walsall, West Bromwich, Dudley and other Black Country areas.

I had passed my promotion examination to Inspector whilst seconded to the Regional Crime Squad. I had also attended two promotion boards but had been unsuccessful. I was not surprised by this but remained ambitious. The small size of Warwickshire gave senior officers the chance to 'black spot' an officer and hold back his career for many years. The West Midlands being some eight times larger than Warwickshire was likely to be more fair and personalities would count for little. I opted for the West Midlands.

The change had little day-to-day effect to begin with, as the personnel changes at senior level were at headquarters and the divisional headquarters level. I did not move job or station on amalgamation. I applied for promotion and on the second series of boards was successful in being selected for promotion to Inspector in early 1976. I had no idea where the posting would be but assumed I would have to move house as I was living in my own home at Nuneaton in Warwickshire. Any posting would have to be further away from Nuneaton due to the geography of the West Midlands. I awaited my fate.

Triumph motorcars provided some light relief both at their motorcar factory and their now redundant motorcycle plant at Meriden.

The car plant had its own security headed by a former Coventry DS, Jock Speed. He dealt with most problems himself, but resorted to calling for our assistance when he felt the offender was persistent or a threat to good working relationships in the plant. An example of the latter was where a patrolling security officer discovered an ingenious method of stealing petrol from parked motorcars. There had been a number of complaints from employees, that their petrol tanks had been emptied whilst in the company car park, resulting in them being unable either to start or to reach home without breaking down. Observations had failed to detect syphoning petrol during working hours and preventive patrols had been

95

introduced to combat the problem. A patrolling security officer noticed a pipe protruding from a petrol cap of one car leading into the boot of another parked adjacent to it. Examination revealed an electric pump in the boot of one car pumping fuel from one car to the other. The offender was interviewed and said that he had not bought any petrol for over two years! He was fined and also dismissed.

An example of the former problem was where Jock had suspected an employee for some time of stealing car parts and had been unable to catch him in possession. One day he caught him with a substantial amount of small parts for a motorcar in current production. We were called in order that his house and garage could be searched. The man lived at Princethorpe and I can say that the Johnny Cash song 'one piece at a time' is true. This man had virtually built a Triumph Dolomite. All that was missing was the bonnet!

There were also many examples of kleptomania where we would find thousands of items stored in methodical fashion in garages and workshops. Items which could not be sold and which had no use whatsoever. There were others who stole to order: batteries, brakes anything at all that would fit in a holdall or even a car. It was amazing how much of it got out; the workers were extremely inventive and the losses enormous.

The Triumph Motorcycle failure was a tragedy and manufacture had continued on a small scale for some time through a workers' co-operative. This had dwindled to where there was a small workforce in occupation of the factory containing completed machines and spares. There were occasional thefts of completed machines, allegedly by burglary. After one such theft, it was clear from a trail left that the motorcycle had been taken out through the rear of the premises to fields beyond. Enquiries revealed that members of the workers' co-operative had been seen wheeling a machine in the field. We were unable to obtain positive identification, but I made it very plain to the workers' leader that any repetition would lead to an anonymous disclosure of the circumstances to the press, thus losing them the public sympathy they cherished. They had no doubt been selling the odd machine, to keep themselves going. I had sympathy for their plight, but it was a crime no less. There was no repetition.

Promotion to Inspector! The list was out and I was posted in uniform to 'L1' Subdivision which was Solihull. There was much to be done. Firstly, to be seen by Sir Philip Knights in order to be formally promoted. This took place in his office on the seventh floor of Lloyd House, the West Midlands Headquarters. There was a considerable number of us, about a dozen I think. We were given a pep talk. The two parts that stick in my memory are: 'Uniform Inspectors on shifts are the most important command level in the force. As duty officer they must deal with everything as it occurs. Decisions are immediate and not made with the benefit of hindsight.' The second was that we would never be in trouble with the Chief Constable for making a wrong decision, but only for making no decision. Brave words – I hoped that they were correct.

There was then the question of uniform and housing. The first was easily resolved, a visit to the clothing store at Bournville would provide the many pairs of trousers, shirts, ties, tunics, raincoats and caps. The second was not so easy. I was living in my own three-bedroom detached house overlooking fields at Nuneaton. A comparable house at Solihull was out of my reach financially – the price difference between Nuneaton and Solihull was and still is considerable. I saw no point in lowering our standards and enquired as to the availability of police houses in Solihull. I was offered a choice of eleven. The choice necessitated a number of journeys with my wife, seven-year-old and six-month-old daughters to look at police houses. We eventually decided to move temporarily to a police house whilst looking for a suitable property to purchase. The temporary occupation of a four-bedroom detached house in Solihull was to last sixteen years!

Chapter Twelve

Uniform Inspector

The promotion was effective from 1 March 1976, but the house move would not take place for two months. I commuted the sixteen miles to Solihull on a daily basis. No great hardship but I was to return to shifts after a gap of nine years. The shifts were 6am–2pm, 2pm–10pm and 10pm–6am. As Inspector I was required to be fully briefed by my predecessor in order to brief my own shift. This meant that I had to be at Solihull for 5.30am on the early shift. I could not wait to move nearer to work.

My first few days of duty were on day shift for familiarisation purposes. One of the first tasks was to be seen and briefed by the Chief Superintendent as to his view of policing the division.

I knew that Solihull was still run on County lines. The public came first, especially the wealthy and influential end of the social strata. It was well known that the 'right' people could obtain a motorcycle escort for the bridal car at their daughter's wedding. Solihull was known as a 'quiet patch' with little trouble. This view was confirmed by the Chief Superintendent, Fred Bunting, a big man with an imposing presence and a twinkling eye. He was a bluff personality and stamped hard on anyone upsetting his particular apple cart. He welcomed me, knew my CID background and assumed quite rightly that I would be looking for an early transfer back to CID. He asked me to give the new job a 'year or two' and that I would find it very rewarding and a pleasant posting. Mr Bunting explained that his main policy was to keep the letters of appreciation 'up here', lifting his hand two feet from the desk and the letters of complaint 'down here', holding his palm just above the surface of the desk. He amused me then, and he amuses me still. I occasionally see him and he introduces me as 'one of my Inspectors' despite the fact that I achieved the same rank as he did!

I took command of my shift for a tour of night duty. I had two outside Sergeants and two inside. The two outside Sergeants were opposites, a young keen ex-Birmingham officer, now sadly dead, and my mentor from the days as a cadet at Nuneaton, Bob Murphy. Nights was an ideal chance to get to know the subdivision and the personnel. I decided to attend as many incidents as possible in order to assess standards and efficiency at first hand. I could not resist interfering however.

The first night I turned up at the Prince of Wales public house where two men were refusing to quit. I arrived to find two PCs arguing with two men. The men had been asked to leave by the licensee and had refused to do so, the PC had told them to leave and they said that they would finish their drinks first, but they made no effort to do so. The licensee was nowhere to be seen. I sent for him and instructed him to repeat his request for the men to leave. He did so and they refused.

I said, 'You have failed to quit licensed premises on being asked by the licensee. You will be ejected.'

I told my PCs to eject them and they did so but when outside the men became abusive and I ordered my officers to arrest them for being drunk and disorderly. This was on Monday night.

On Tuesday night, I attended a disturbance at another public house and ordered the arrest of another man for being drunk and disorderly.

I arrived for duty at 9.30pm on the Wednesday evening

and there waiting for me in the control room was the Chief Superintendent.

He said, 'Now Inspector, what has been going on? Why are there three prisoners arrested for being drunk and disorderly in two nights?'

I said, 'The men were drunk and they were disorderly.'

'I know that Inspector,' said the Chief Superintendent. 'What I mean is, how is it that we only had eleven such cases in the whole of last year and you have had three in two days? I have to report to the Brewster sessions. The magistrates will think we cannot keep control.'

'But that's what I'm doing,' I said. 'Am I supposed to ignore it?'

'No,' he said. 'Ways and means, caution, have them taken home. Remember, complaints down here, compliments up there,' said he moving his hand up and down. 'Meaning clear?'

'Oh yes, sir, very,' I replied.

I tried not to upset him too much over the next year or so, but ensured that order was kept when my shift were on duty.

I had begun to settle in well and had arranged my house move when I received notice that I was to attend the Inspectors' course at the Police Staff College at Bramshill in Hampshire. The course was in two parts: a regional element of two months based at Tally Ho! Police training centre in Birmingham and then a further four months at Bramshill. The Police College was considered to be the acme of police training and a goal for any ambitious officer. There was no possibility of promotion beyond Inspector without successfully attending the Inspectors' course. The course was residential with weekend leave from Friday evening to Sunday evening. My wife was thrilled! I moved her and the girls into a new house in a strange town and then left her for six months!

The first two months at Tally Ho! were very interesting and stimulating. There were two directors of studies, both

100

high flyers, one from the West Midlands and the other from West Mercia. The students were from West Midlands, West Mercia and Staffordshire. We were a small group and the tuition was geared to professional subjects. I felt that we learned a lot. I was not alone in thinking that two months was probably more than sufficient for our needs, and yet we were now to undertake a further four-month course of study.

We had been briefed that the Police College would be a combination of academic and professional studies and that we would be required to select an academic and a professional specialism. I sought out one or two former students of my acquaintance in order to pick up tips on protocol, personalities, pubs and advice on work and workloads. I was told that Bramshill was 'Butlin's with essays' – in other words a holiday camp with some written work. I was given much advice which proved invaluable.

One of the myths of Bramshill was that future senior officers were taught how to eat and drink properly at social events. Certainly there were formal guest nights, but no instructions in cutlery and cruet.

The Police College is based in and around a Tudor mansion near Hartley Wintney in Hampshire. It is impressive in appearance and approached by an even more impressive drive.

We arrived on a Sunday afternoon and were allocated rooms and syndicates. We were introduced to our professional syndicate director, a policeman. Mine was to be my old adversary from the Henley murder, Jock Shaw, who was now a Superintendent. Not a promising start. We were shown our syndicate room and told to report there the following morning after breakfast.

Monday morning arrived and we assembled in the classroom. We were syndicate 9, one of a dozen syndicates of fourteen officers, a large group from all Forces in England and Wales. All students were in uniform, including the DIs. Some did not look very comfortable in their blue serge. We

101

were introduced to our academic director, John Rhind, my idea of an academic, beard and sandals. Pep talks were given, details of essay requirements, behaviour standards and rules of the college. Certain pubs were named as 'out of bounds', a certainty for a visit. 'Monitors' jobs were given out.

Then came the important selection of specialisms. The whole of Monday each week was given up to the academic specialism and half a day of each week to the professional version. I had already selected community policing as my professional specialism and had been strongly advised to opt for Language and Literature as my academic choice. I indicated my options and learned later in the week that I had been successful in obtaining both my choices.

The first Monday of Language and Literature arrived. I had been well briefed as to what would occur. The first hour of each Monday would be given over to a talk on an author or poet by one of the two tutors, Major Roddick and Captain Walker, two delightful old soldiers. One had Indian Army experience and the other Arabic experiences. The remainder of the day was given over to reading the selected works of a specific author on which one was required to present a paper to the rest of the group.

The selection of the author was made at a meeting with Major Roddick. My advisor told me to be vague, but to express an interest in India. He said that I was certain to be given John Masters, the author of Bhowani Junction, as the Major was a huge fan. I followed the advice and sure enough was allocated John Masters. There followed three months of Mondays of total bliss – this was the outstanding summer of 1976 and I was able to spend all day sitting by the lake reading the excellent novels of John Masters.

I presented a paper on the author with particular reference to *The Night Runners of Bengal*, an account of the Indian Mutiny. It was well received by students and tutors alike. As Major Roddick wrote on my report, 'the object was achieved' – more than he knew!

I repeated the advice on Language and Literature to my old friend from Rugby, Keith Longcroft who was on the course following mine. The ploy worked well including the bonus that he was able to use my written paper. He received complimentary remarks from the Major.

The course was a wonderful experience, but much of it was a complete waste of time. The course had been running to the same format for many years and no-one seemed to be stretched. It was a very amiable club, there was plenty of sport, I became very fit and proficient at volleyball and badminton. There were long summer evenings in a delightful part of the country. There were many pubs in the area, but those in the immediate vicinity were full of policemen and the landlords were not easily persuaded to 'George Rafters' – drinks after time.

I became friendly early on with a DI from the Met, Tommy Hamilton. We hit it off on the first Monday night when we were all as a syndicate invited to John Rhind's house, a converted barn in a nearby village. It was all a bit stilted and there was only wine to drink and I was a committed beer drinker. I saw that Tommy was restless and suggested that we nip out to the pub across the road. He agreed. I said to John Rhind, 'Just popping out for some cigarettes.'

'And me,' said Tommy. We were soon ensconced with a pint of bitter each and it was not too long before we were joined by others.

After about an hour, Jock Shaw came in and said, 'Out! All of you. There are only five of us across the road. I suppose this is down to you Mr Hannis.' I ignored him.

Tommy and I decided to explore the area around the college. I said that all the old hostelries were marked on the Ordnance Survey map and that we should visit the college library and borrow one. This we did one evening and the following day Jock Shaw announced to the group, 'Things are looking up. I hear that Mr Hamilton and Mr Hannis have decided to take the course seriously; they were seen in the library last night.' He laughed, good-naturedly.

I said, 'Don't worry sir, we were only getting an Ordnance Survey map to find all the old pubs.' He didn't laugh then.

Despite my levity and minor acts of rebelliousness, I completed all my assignments and received a good report at the end of the course. The report went down well at Lloyd House and was not to impede my future career.

I returned to Solihull bursting with knowledge and certainly with increased confidence. There had been some personnel changes on my shift during my absence and also changes in management at Superintendent level. The work seemed unaffected and it was certainly no busier than when I left.

Mr Bunting was still in charge and still running a quiet and steady ship. The Licensing Inspector, Ernie Barnett, was to retire. His job was something of a sinecure, with considerable social benefits. The post was not too demanding as Ernie was also treasurer of Solihull police club and the Inspectors' Representative of the Police Federation for the Division. The latter was no problem; L division was not known for its militancy. The former, however, was a demanding and time-consuming task requiring much off duty commitment. The labours included VAT returns, Income Tax, National Insurance, Gaming Machinery receipts and the keeping of the club accounts.

The licensing post was much sought after: no shifts, your own boss and invited to numerous dinners, lunches, balls, golf and like events. There was considerable jockeying for position, but I was not a runner, I had no interest in licensing apart from visiting the pub.

The appointment was made so I was surprised to be summoned by the Chief Superintendent to discuss Ernie Barnett's retirement. 'You know that Mr Barnett is retiring?'

'Of course,' I said in reply to the Chief Superintendent's greeting.

'Well, I want you to be the club treasurer and the

Federation Representative. What do you say?'

I said, 'But these are elected positions. The club members and the Inspectors have to vote.'

The Chief Superintendent said, 'I've elected you. I'm not having some PC handling all that money in the club. You can do it.'

'But what about the Federation?' I said.

'It's all right, its only nominal, no-one's interested. You just go to the meetings. I have every confidence in you and I'm sure that you will do well.'

I recognised the implied threat and accepted the generous offer.

Solihull began to go downhill from then on. I became more and more frustrated with the treasurer's job – it was a thankless task and I began to intensely dislike keeping the books. The police work was not challenging and I began to look for a way out.

CID vacancies at DI level were difficult to get – you needed a sponsor and at that time I did not have one. It was by now the late summer of 1978 and I noticed an advertisement in *Force Orders* for Instructors at the Detective Training School at Tally Ho! The position was for two years as a DI and a good posting from where to find a sponsor for a CID position at the end of the attachment. My only lecturing experience had been during my Inspectors' course where we were required to deliver a number of lectures throughout the six months. I had enjoyed the experience and thought I could become proficient at it.

I duly applied and was called for an interview at Tally Ho! The interview panel was Harry Robinson, the ACC (Crime) and Brian Martindale, the DCI in charge of the Detective Training School together with the Chief Superintendent Training. The interview was thorough and it was stressed that there were no immediate vacancies, but they were planning ahead. It was a pre-requisite that any instructor attend the eight-week course for student instructors at the Central Planning and Instructor Training Unit at

Pannal Ash, Harrogate. Passing the course would ensure future selection as an instructor.

I was informed that I had been successful at interview and that I was to attend an eight-week course running from December 1978 to February 1979. I was elated, wife was not so thrilled: another two months away with only two days at home each week.

Chapter Thirteen

Detective Training

The Instructor Training Unit was geared to producing instructors of sufficient standard to teach at District Training Centres, where recruits were trained, and officers for uniform In-Force Training. Detective Training Schools did not fit into their system in that instruction was not geared to detectives who needed to learn criminal law in depth together with relative practice and procedure for criminal investigations. My training was geared to qualify me to teach at a District Training Centre.

I was an unusual animal in that in addition to being a detective, I was also an Inspector. Normally, students were Constables and Sergeants. This was not a problem at Harrogate but did become one at the District Training Centre when I undertook my teaching practice, which was also a final assessment as to suitability to work as an instructor.

The instructors at Harrogate were all highly-trained policemen, trained at an educational establishment in the civilian sector. The training given to us was intensive and intentionally stressful. Six weeks' training was to take us from basic methods of presentation to the delivery of fifty-minute periods of law instruction. The method was simple 'talk and chalk': verbal presentation supported by overhead projection and chalk or dry-wipe boards. It was reckoned that a fifty-minute presentation required seven hours of preparation. The motto was 'failing to plan is planning to fail', a motto much used by me in later years.

There was preparation each evening for presentation the following day and to add insult to injury, we were given a presentation title on Friday afternoons for presentation on Mondays.

I found the preparation laborious, though not difficult, and the presentation stressful. I could not relax; the parameters were too rigid for me. I persevered, however, and eventually teaching practice arrived.

I was to undertake two weeks' teaching practice at the No4 District Police Training Centre at Ryton-on-Dunsmore where I had undergone my initial training.

The subjects for presentation were not given until arrival at the centre. The presentations were to be made to recruits in training and it was emphasised that appearance was very important as high standards of turnout were required. I had been required to remove my sideburns as it was suggested that if I was a success all the males would grow them. I doubted that, but shaved them off anyway.

An assessor was appointed who would sit in on all my lectures. Mine was an experienced woman Inspector from the north east. She seemed somewhat dour. I was also to be assessed by my Instructor from Harrogate, Bobby Bach.

I began my teaching practice: traffic law, pedlars, but no criminal law! My preparation was difficult, due to the lack of knowledge on my part. I also realised that as an Inspector the recruits were hanging on my every word. I had to be right!

By the end of my first week, Christine Gowland, my assessor said to me, 'You're not enjoying this are you?'

'No,' I admitted. 'If it doesn't improve I won't be taking it up as a job.'

She said, 'And I'd support you.' But why are you not funny, as you are outside the class?'

'I have to stick to the syllabus there is no room for manoeuvre,' I replied.

'You're wrong', said Christine. 'Be yourself. Cover the syllabus, but be yourself.'

The following week I changed my approach and dealt with the recruits as I would have dealt with any personnel. It worked! At the end of a period on metal dealers, Christine said, 'The CID are going to bless you, the first thing these kids are going to do when they get out on their own is check metal dealers' books and yards.' A successful presentation, I thought.

I was, however, due for a fall – and I got one. I was given a double period, two fifty-minute sessions, on the use of and the law relating to breathalysers. I had not used one and was not a convert to its use. I was singularly unqualified to teach the subject. I did my homework and began the lecture.

I said, 'You are particularly fortunate today to have before you an expert on the breathalyser – an expert in avoiding them. I have never used one in anger and indeed never assembled one. We will all learn together.'

Christine had her head in her hands.

The lesson was going quite well until 'Harvey' started; there was one in every class. 'What about Rv so-and-so sir?' and 'Doesn't Rv thing say the opposite sir?' I was out of my depth and said, 'Come on son, you come out here and I'll sit down.'

Disaster! Failure loomed. It transpired however that what I had taught, the students had remembered: some even said they would 'never forget it'!

I passed and in fact was graded well. I now had to wait for a vacancy at Tally Ho! and until then I was to resume my duties at Solihull. I was by now very unsettled. I was ready for a move, but it seemed there was no projected vacancy until August and it was only February.

Within a week or two of my return, I was summoned by the Superintendent. It transpired that an Instructor at the Detective Training School was not performing well and I was to take up post immediately. I was very pleased – a quick farewell drink in the club with my shift and I was off. I firmly believe that it was the best decision I made in the job. The move was to give me huge personal confidence and open a number of doors as well as providing me with a mentor at senior level.

Tally Ho! was a Home Office Detective Training School, one of a number in England covering training requirements for England, Wales and Northern Ireland.

I arrived in the middle of term. There were four terms a year at the Detective Training School: each consisted of a ten-week junior course for officers recently appointed to CID or officers selected for CID, with a proviso that they must pass the course. This pass was a fifty per cent minimum in the written examination and a satisfactory report. There was also a three-week refresher course in weeks one to three and a six-week advanced course in weeks five to ten, which ran parallel to the junior course. The refresher course was for experienced CID officers: to update them on the criminal law and advances in investigative techniques. The advanced course was for Detective Sergeants and DIs. It was essentially a refresher and update together with information on investigative techniques and scientific support.

The courses were intensive and demanding but only the junior course were subjected to examination.

Having arrived after the start of the junior course, I was placed in charge of an advanced course of a dozen experienced and cynical senior detectives of Sergeant and Inspector rank, which was no problem as I was one myself. The problem was that I was to teach them the law. My predecessor had been asked to leave due to his inability to move from the lectern and his notes, which both make for an extremely boring input.

Brian Martindale, the DCI, knew that I was under some pressure, as my first input was to be six hours on sexual offences to the advanced course. This required some forty hours of preparation. Brian kindly took over my supervisory responsibilities whilst I prepared my notes.

110

The great day arrived. I was to deliver the whole six hours in one day. A new boy, a new subject, a new environment and an old cynical audience. It went surprisingly well, I knew my subject and felt relatively easy with my audience. I was not subject to assessment by my superiors, but at the end of the six hours all the class held up two cards with marks out of six as in the skating arena. I did not add them up, but I am sure it was not 6.6.6.6.6.6.6.6!

The whole syllabus was divided between the instructors, including the DCI. There were three DIs and three DSs as there were two junior classes of twenty-plus students in addition to the refresher and advanced courses. The allocated subjects were taught by each instructor to all the courses. It was a busy time: it was essential to keep fully up-to-date with law and practical matters as the credibility of the school was that all the staff were experienced detectives. To ensure that credibility no-one was allowed to stay more than two years.

The courses were residential and there was a need to arrange some evening activities, always involving drink! The final week was one long round of 'final dos'. I soon learned to pack a suitcase on the Monday of the final week so that I could stay over and go home on Friday evening. No driving during the week was then necessary!

The syllabus contained many practical inputs such as surveillance training, scene examination, identification exercises, a murder day and informative lectures from pathologists, police surgeons, odontologists, forensic scientists, customs and excise, fingerprint experts, Special Branch and immigration. In fact every facet of crime investigation and detection was covered, including court presentation from practising barristers. It was a most enjoyable course from the students' point of view and a much sought-after experience.

There were inevitably problems from time to time with the resident students – usually drink or women or both. There was no lasting damage however and it was very rare for an officer to return to his force for misconduct. The threat of such action was normally enough to prevent a recurrence of the misconduct by the individual. There were a number of 'out of bounds' premises and these were strictly enforced. Birmingham was a major city with many inherent dangers, especially for officers from more rural areas.

There were many characters on the staff and amongst the students. There were also great characters amongst the visiting lecturers, not least of whom was Dr Ben Davies, the Home Office Pathologist. He was very experienced and hugely enjoyed his work. His input to the junior courses, with whom he had two full afternoons of presentation, was very entertaining. He took great delight in showing particularly gory slides and was always most amused when someone fainted or had to leave the room. He drove an old Morris Minor 1000 and was completely imperturbable. He was always invited to 'final dos' and attended when his duties permitted. There was one occasion at a 'final do' of the junior course, where a stripper had been primed to go and sit on Dr Ben's lap. As she did so some wag shouted, 'What are they like when they're warm doc?'

And another: 'Give him a knife, he'll feel more at home.'

I soon settled into my role and found my sense of humour a great advantage, but I did tend to go a little over the top sometimes, especially when introducing some of the visitors. Our police surgeon was Dr Targett, a very pleasant young doctor, now sadly no longer with us. I introduced him as, 'A very competent police surgeon with flashes of brilliance – which is illustrated by his ability to keep the Aston Villa football team playing every week.' He was the Villa doctor and I follow Coventry City.

One of my favourite visitors was Bob Paradis, a Sergeant in the Royal Canadian Mounted Police attached to the Canadian High Commission in London. It was the DCI's policy to have an entertaining input on the Friday afternoon to send the troops off happy to their wives and girlfriends. Bob would come late morning and take lunch before his talk and on occasions arrive on Thursday afternoons and spend the evening with us. He was a very handsome and personable man and I always wound up the students, especially the girls, that he would be in uniform – big hat, red coat, leather boots, the full works. I would ask him to remain outside the lecture theatre whilst making my introduction and I would finish by singing 'Rose Marie' – and then in he would come with blue suit and white shirt. Juvenile, but always funny.

Examinations were a problem. It was essential to test the students' level of knowledge. Tests were also needed to ensure that everyone worked properly, and they were also demanded by the home forces to assess the potential of their officers. Each instructor set questions on his own areas of specialism. The demands of questions were therefore variable and it was also open to an instructor to 'coach' his class in order to obtain good results. There were a number of complaints of favouritism, usually from students who had done badly, to their senior officers back at force, when interviewed regarding their course report. Some of these complaints alleged that Masonic influences had been at work. The result was a change in the system and an opportunity for a 'wind-up'.

The new policy was that each instructor would set a number of questions on each of his subjects and these would be put into a bank from which the DCI would select questions to compile the examination papers.

I decided to take action on the 'Masonic' allegation. Masonry has always been a bone of contention within the police service and the issue has still not been satisfactorily resolved. I was acting DCI and issued a memo that any member of staff who was a member of a secret society must suspend his membership during his attachment to the Detective Training School or else return to his normal duty. I knew that this would cause a problem to one of the

113

Sergeants and sure enough he came to me and asked to speak in confidence. 'Of course,' I said.

He told me that he had been elected secretary of his lodge and could not relinquish such a post but as he was also qualified for promotion, he could not leave the Detective Training School. What to do? I told him, 'If you hadn't done so much typing for the lodge at work I would never have known, so I put the memo out as a joke.'

He was furious that I had not only conned him into telling me of his role in the lodge, but also that he had come to me for advice!

The time at Tally Ho! was to open many doors to me, mainly through meeting senior officers who came to speak to courses or attend meetings. There is no doubt that my main sponsor was David Gerty, a Metropolitan Senior Detective appointed as Assistant Chief Constable (Crime) following the retirement of Harry Robinson. Mr Gerty needed to find a house in the West Midlands and in the interim he lived at Tally Ho! In his free time he graduated towards the only detectives in the building, the instructors at the training school. He and I hit it off and became friendly on a social level. The work level was a huge gap from DI to ACC and I was always extremely respectful. There were no obvious benefits from the relationship but no obvious draw-backs either!

One of the matters Mr Gerty discussed with me was training in interview or interrogation. The interviewing of prisoners, suspects and witnesses was an extremely important part of a detective's work, but no training whatsoever was given in the interviewing of prisoners and suspects. Detectives considered it to be an 'art' and a 'natural ability' that could not be taught. In truth the training was 'on the job': learning by picking up techniques from others, whether good or bad. The only constraint was to stay within the law or not get caught.

Mr Gerty believed that there was potential to create 'interrogation' squads: teams of officers who would be trained in interview technique and deal with all prisoners at interview stage. He believed that it would achieve better results and provide admissible evidence. It would also reduce the number of complaints. The theory was sound, but who was going to teach the technique? Who was going to write the course?

Mr Gerty was aware that the Armed Services had an Interrogation Training Wing which trained personnel to act as interrogators in time of war. The suitability of such a course for the police was unknown and needed to be investigated. Permission was obtained from the Ministry of Defence to send three West Midland Officers on the Long Interrogation Course at the Joint Services Interrogation Wing (JSIW) at Ashford in Kent.

Three officers were selected: me, as a trainer; DCI Roy Taylor – officer in charge of the West Midlands Serious Crime Squad, the group of detectives interviewing the most hardened criminals in the Midlands; and DI John Dagley, Special Branch, a department with the potential to be interviewing terrorists. Our brief was to fully participate in the course, not to be observers, and then report upon its value and potential to the police. In addition, I was tasked with writing a paper on the training and use of 'Interrogation Squads'.

We reported to Ashford on a Sunday evening. The course was three weeks and run by a Lieutenant Colonel with the day-to-day responsibility in the hands of a Major. Both men were Intelligence Corps officers. The students were from all three Services and the American Air Force. Ranks varied from Corporal to Captain. We were installed in the officers' mess, John and I with the rank of Lieutenant and Roy as a Captain.

The course was in two parts: two weeks at Ashford receiving instruction and practising the lessons, and a week of practical testing elsewhere.

The course was remarkable. People who had never interviewed anyone were taught to be competent interrogators.

The problem for us as policeman was that there were no Judges Rules to restrict questions. If the 'prisoner' was in a war-time scenario, we were only ever going to get name, rank and number. Despite the restrictions, we all found the course enjoyable and were convinced that interviewing could be taught.

At the end of the fortnight we had a couple of days at home and then reported to the SAS at Pontrilas in the Welsh Borders. This was to be our examination!

We were to be part of an assessment course for SAS and SBS candidates. The candidates had been cast adrift in wild country without food, proper clothing or conventional means of obtaining food. They had to survive without committing crime and evade capture. As part of the exercise they were required to make a number of rendezvous points and at one of these they were captured and taken blindfolded to Pontrilas. They were hooded and subjected to sensory deprivation. From time to time they would be taken to an interrogation room where they would be interviewed by us!

The interrogation rooms were all identical, with no numbers, and no clocks. We all wore identical clothes and no watches. We were required to interview the candidates as we had been taught and we were not allowed to touch the candidates at all.

I was paired with John Dagley and we soon found it irksome as we were getting no reaction other than name, rank, number and 'I cannot answer that question'. The candidates were very tough men and our methods were clearly not going to trouble them. We decided to vary the technique. We had notes from their earlier interviews together with full personal descriptions, including tattoos. We began to use two different methods: personal abuse relating to their appearance – tattoos or something else relating to them – and laughter, by posing questions which when receiving one of the four replies they were allowed to give, sounded ridiculous. We knew that if the candidates reacted by assaulting us, they would fail, so we were not being particularly brave, just grossly unfair. It was a war scenario!

To begin with, we were congratulated on our novel approach, but then one candidate broke down and asked to be withdrawn from the course. Soon afterwards a second candidate failed to survive our punishing and abusive questioning. We were hauled in front of a very large and rather frightening SAS Colonel who told us to restrict ourselves to the standard methods of questioning. Suitably chastised, we reverted to the less stressful form of questioning.

It was a wonderful experience and we viewed it as a unique opportunity to adapt armed services' training to civilian policing. Interview training did not become an essential part of police training for a number of years however.

In the late spring of 1979 an unusual opportunity was presented to me. John Glyn, the Assistant Chief Constable Personnel and Training, to whom I was responsible as a member of the Training Department, asked me to apply for a Scholarship to Cambridge! It was not as grand as it first sounded, but was nevertheless an exciting prospect.

Wolfson College, Cambridge, formerly University College, had long run a course for Managers in Industry and Commerce to give non-graduates with Senior Management potential the experience of university life. The course had originally included a police officer, but due to lack of funding, this had lapsed. The college had persuaded the Midland Bank to sponsor a police officer each term and I was to apply on behalf of the West Midlands Police for the year 1979/80.

This being a new sponsorship and no one from the West Midlands having ever attended the previous police studentship, little was known of what was required. The information leaflet indicated that there was a core course and the successful applicant would be expected to study a subject of their own choice in addition. The sponsorship was for one term.

The ACC told me that I had been selected as someone who could benefit from the course and cope with it intellectually! My ten 'O' levels and one 'A' level had come in handy. I thought that my selection also indicated that I was well thought of at HQ and decided to apply. I stressed in my application a long-held interest in English Literature and a desire to experience university life. As the only applicant, the force strongly recommended me!

I was short-listed and called for interview at Cambridge. I was extremely apprehensive when I arrived at Wolfson. This was an unknown area for me – a great seat of learning and an interview by noted academics was a very daunting prospect. The secretary, Judy Lowe, was very pleasant and tried to put me at ease. I was called to the interview room where I expected two or three academics, but it was a much larger gathering. It was something like 'when did you last see your father', the civil war painting: an open rectangle with a solitary chair for me at the open end.

The board were introduced: the President of the College, the Course Director and College Bursar, Jack King, a Senior Fellow, Bill Kirkham, a Director of the Midland Bank, two more college Fellows and last but not least, the Chief Constable of Cambridgeshire, Vic Gilbert.

I cannot remember the majority of the questions, but felt that I was floundering until someone, not the Chief Constable, asked me a question on policing. I was away: I treated them like a class, eye contact with all, used my hands and when they follow them, you know you've got them. I was fine until one Fellow asked me which author I intended to study if I was successful. I had no idea and began to waffle! Jack King stepped right in to help. 'How can he know when he has no idea what the *Reporter* will offer?'

I nodded, not knowing what the *Reporter* was.

The President said, 'Yes, let him decide when the *Reporter* is published.'

I thought, 'I've got this!'

118

I was then dismissed but was invited to wait to have lunch, but I could not wait to get out and stop at a pub for a pint!

Within a few weeks, I learned that I had been successful. I opted for the Lent Term which would be spring in Cambridge. Ten weeks as a student! I could not wait and my long-suffering wife agreed that I should not come home for the period and that she would visit from time to time.

There were a number of formalities before I took up my place. I was to spend a day at Wolfson, mainly to decide upon my subject. I learned on arrival what the *Cambridge Reporter* would show me: all activities in the academic life of the university. English Literature for Lent offered lectures, classes and seminars on Thomas Hardy. I was very familiar with *Far from the Madding Crowd*, and *The Mayor of Casterbridge* and was very happy to opt to study Hardy for my one term. I enjoyed a good lunch with Jack and returned to Birmingham full of anticipation for January 1980.

There were two tasks to complete before my student life began. The first was to continue my instructor role and the second and more important was to find myself a job. My two years at Tally Ho! would expire during the coming Lent term and it was essential to find a posting before then. I was determined to stay in the CID and began some lobbying. One of the people I lobbied was my former DCI at Tally Ho!, Brian Martindale. He was now a DCI in Special Branch and as a former member of the Birmingham City Serious Crime Squad, he was not without influence. My impending ten week absence was not conducive to being considered an attractive candidate by Operational Detective Superintendents.

There were regular conferences of CID supervisory officers, known as 'DIs and CIs' meetings. These were dual-purpose meetings: an information exchange and a chance for senior officers to 'lay down the law' to Inspectors and Chief Inspectors. As a non-operational unit the Detective Training School were only represented by the DCI, Ray Dyde.

On the morning of one conference, Ray Dyde said to me, 'Bill, I can't go to DIs and CIs today. You go. It's at Stechford.' I was pleased to accept as I thought it might be an opportunity to further my cause as a DI.

Conference was always followed by a buffet lunch and considerable drink – a team-building session it would be called these days, if drink was allowed! Brian Martindale called to me, 'I've got you a place at our table Bill.' I joined Brian and a number of other officers, some of whom I recognised. One was the head of Special Branch, Superintendent McCaughey. There were two other DCIs from Special Branch in addition to Brian at the table. We had an enjoyable lunch with a lively and varied conversation.

When we had finished eating, I excused myself and went to the toilet. I was standing at the urinal when Superintendent McCaughey came in and stood next to me. 'I hear that you'd like to join us,' he said.

'Join what?' I said, thinking, 'What is going on here?'

'Special Branch,' said Mr McCaughey.

'Oh yes, very much,' I said.

'Well you're in. It will be in orders. Well done,' said the Superintendent.

I was pleased he did not offer me his hand! I knew Special Branch was secret, but I thought this was taking things a bit far.

I returned to the table where Mr McCaughey announced that I was joining Special Branch. A knowing smile from Brian and a very broad grin from Ray when I got back to Tally Ho!

Problem solved. The transfer was arranged quickly to give me time to settle in to the Special Branch before going off to Cambridge.

Chapter Fourteen

Special Branch and Cambridge

I knew little of Special Branch work other than that they were responsible for Immigration and Nationality, Anti-Terrorism, an Airport unit and the broad area of 'anti subversion'. I had no knowledge of their methods or personnel other than John Dagley of the Ashford course. I had not visited their offices which were in the headquarters at Lloyd House in Birmingham.

Superintendent McCaughey informed me that a parking space would be available for me on my first day and that I should speak to Lloyd House reception staff to gain admission to the car park. I was expected in the office at 9am.

I arrived in plenty of time on my first morning and duly presented myself at reception where I was met by the owner of the car park, at least that's how he behaved, an unfriendly Sergeant who consulted lists and made a telephone call before making the necessary arrangements for me to park. I was now late! I arrived at the Special Branch office door, where one was required to ring a bell to gain admission, in something of a fluster.

I was admitted to find Superintendent McCaughey, three DCIs, including Brian Martindale and an Inspector all standing in a line to greet me.

'Good morning,' I said, 'I'm sorry to be a minute or two late, but I had problems parking. Some bossy Sergeant thought he owned the place.'

'Oh, that will be Dennis,' said Mr McCaughey with a smile.

'What, Mick's dad?' said I, he being the father of my Sergeant from Tally Ho!

'Yes,' said the Superintendent.

'Well, if I had known that, I would have rolled up my trouser leg and bared my chest. I'd have been in then,' I said laughing.

No response.

'You know,' I continued blithely, 'he's a mason. I think he's a Wizard.'

Still no response apart from a shake of the head from Brian Martindale who told me later that all, apart from him, were Freemasons. What a start!

I was put in charge of what was called 'the left wing'. It was a wider brief than that and my first few days were spent reading to familiarise myself with all the areas covered by my staff. These ranged from monitoring the activities of the 'normal' Communist groups to the extreme revolutionary cells, covering meetings, infiltrating organisations, surveillance of individuals and many 'secret agents'. I was also performing normal supervisory tasks during this time. I was amazed. My mouth was open most of the time. I had no idea such work was undertaken and clearly I cannot expand on it here, as I am still restricted by the Official Secrets Act. Suffice to say that there was a much greater danger to the democracy and the security of our country than I had ever imagined. I was very naive in many areas and must have been something of a surprise to my subordinates in my lack of knowledge. I was however becoming known in the force for my pragmatism, something clearly needed on the 'left wing'.

The pedantry involved in the production of reports, especially those for 'Box 500' or MI5 as I knew it, was remarkable. English language classes at grammar school had been less demanding than the production of these reports. I could do little on that as Mr McCaughey and his deputy Phil Padgett were the chief pedants. I could do something, however, about duplication and unnecessary secrecy. The secrecy rule was 'need to know', sounds simple, you were not told if you did not need to know. The trouble was it was applied very rigidly and resulted in duplication of effort. Two officers would be looking at the same area from different angles and not pooling information. I could not understand the reasoning – everyone in the department was 'positively vetted' meaning that active enquiries had been made into backgrounds to eradicate, or at least reduce, the possibility of a security problem. Why therefore could there not be a much wider information exchange? My suggestion fell on stony ground at senior level, but I was in a position to do something about it on the 'left wing'.

I got two of my Detective Sergeants into my office and asked why they did not pool information.

'Need to know, boss,' was the reply.

I was considered something of a nuisance as a non-SB man and the look accompanying the remark implied 'We know you don't understand'.

I cited one glaring example where they were duplicating work. They were surprised and embarrassed, and immediately agreed to rectify that situation. I cited more examples over the next few weeks.

I was then ready for Cambridge. The left wing were probably glad to see the back of me for three months. Mr McCaughey cautioned me before I left as to concealing my current role during my studentship. He said that a DI from Special Branch responsible for left wing matters would not sit too well as a member of the student body at Cambridge. Very wise! It was agreed that I would adopt a role of DI Anti-Terrorist Squad for the term – not far removed, but less controversial.

123

I was ready to go. I had bought a bicycle to use at Cambridge and drove up on a Sunday with my wife and two girls. I had been allocated half a 'set' at Wolfson which I was to share with another member of the course, Charles Flett, a manager from IBM. I unloaded and unpacked and then bid farewell to my three girls, all of us somewhat tearful at the prospect of father being away from home for ten weeks. My wife and I had agreed that this was a unique experience of which I must take full advantage – weekends were part of University life and a Monday to Friday involvement would have lost a lot.

The first day was a full one, meeting fellow students, familiarisation with the College, a briefing on the course and then a tour of the university and its colleges by a blue badge guide who was the wife of one of the Fellows. A very exciting day.

My fellow students were, in addition to Charles Flett, Mike Mitchell, a manager from ICI in Cheshire (now sadly deceased), Mike Shannon, Geoff Pennington and Joe Whetham all from IBM, a Mr Matsui from Tokyo and Geoff Russell from the Midland Bank. A small group, but a lively one.

The course was constructed so that we followed our own subjects in the mornings when university lectures took place. The afternoon was given over to a core course designed to broaden our education: History of Art, Literature, Music, visits to the Fitzwilliam Museum, the Scott Institute and many more activities and lectures in a very varied programme. In addition, there was at least one 'supper' a week where Jack King would invite a speaker to eat with us and address us on his specialist subject during the evening. The subjects ranged from 'The Black Fen' to 'Decorative Wrought Iron Work'.

We were expected to participate fully in college life which included 'dining in' on two nights a week. There was a common table at Wolfson – all college members shared common dining with President, Fellows and students, and there was no high table. At the conclusion of my first 'dining in', on the Tuesday night, I felt that I was totally out of my depth. Jack had supervised our seating on this first night to ensure that we did not all sit together. He separated us and we awaited our fate. None had ever attended university and here we were at Cambridge dining with graduates, undergraduates and Fellows at one of the finest universities in the world. What would the conversation be about?

On my left was Hugh Plommer, a Senior Fellow and Classics Don. He introduced himself and said, 'Are you one of the industrials?'

I said, 'No, I'm a policeman.'

'No, no. I mean, one of Jack's course, we call them industrials,' said Hugh.

'Oh, yes,' I replied.

'Where are you from?' asked Hugh.

'The West Midlands,' I said.

'No. I mean originally. North Warwickshire, I think, somewhere near Atherstone,' said Hugh.

I thought of Professor Higgins – this man had placed my accent within five miles.

'That's amazing,' I said. 'I come from Nuneaton, five miles away.'

'Nuneaton,' mused Hugh. 'I've passed through it on the train, a bloody awful place!' I had no answer. I was somewhat abashed and as the conversation flowed, my contributions were limited to smiles and nods.

'What are you studying while you are here?' demanded a lady Fellow sitting opposite.

'Thomas Hardy,' said I.

'Oh yes, Hardy. I do so love Hardy. The passage from *Tess* where the blood drips through the floor after she has stabbed D'Urbeville is most evocative, don't you think?' said the learned lady.

'Oh yes indeed,' I replied, not having a clue what she was talking about. I had only read *Far from the Madding,*

Casterbridge and *Two On a Tower* and the last one only recently. I had not enjoyed it and wondered if all the other works were similar. I thought 'this is going to be a nightmare'.

Thankfully, I was wrong. These lovely people were not putting me down, they were behaving normally, as I came to learn. They were ever ready to be helpful, explain or assist, but in these early days I was unaware of this.

The academic life was fascinating. I was as a member of the Wolfson course, a full member of the university, no restrictions and every advantage. My 'Thomas Hardy' activities were to be supervised by a tutor. His task was to ensure that I got the most benefit from my classes, lectures and seminars during the term.

I met with my tutor in the first week and he explained that it might be that I would not understand some of the content, an understatement as it turned out, but that he was there to explain. I was to meet with him weekly and discuss my progress. At the first tutorial he gave me *Under the Greenwood Tree*, one of Hardy's slimmer novels. My tutor asked me to try and finish it by the following week. Try! I had no distractions and every encouragement to read and by the following week I was into my third novel and he realised that I was a voracious reader. He then introduced me to a biography of Hardy in addition to continuing the novels.

Week three found me getting somewhat confused at the views of the undergraduates on Hardy's novels. I attended seminars with a man called Barrell, where the students discussed a Hardy novel. I was not expected to participate greatly but to learn from the experience. I had developed a system of writing copious notes in order to both remember and also to have my tutor explain areas I did not understand. My confusion at this stage related to 'phallic symbols' that the students kept seeing in *The Return of the Native*. I thought that Hardy was describing Egdon Heath but they saw it as some repressed sexual feeling! My tutor

126

thought that my notes were hilarious and began to look forward to my weekly visits. He said that my diary of the week in the English faculty gave him a whole new view of the university.

The social side was a very important aspect of selling the Wolfson course and the college. Jack King was College Bursar in addition to being our Course Director. He had been the catalyst for the majority of donations for the college buildings and he often said, 'My blood is on the walls.' To further the reputation of the course and college Jack invited many people to lunch and supper. Wine was an important part of such meals and we did justice to the College's very fine cellar.

One morning Jack said to me, 'Bill, there is a policeman coming to lunch. I'll be delayed, will you look after him for me?'

'Of course,' I said 'who is he?'

'One of your chaps – Vic Gilbert. Gin and tonic, large,' said Jack.

'But he's the Chief Constable,' I protested.

'Yes, a policeman, as you are. You'll be fine.'

Jack was a great friend of the police and we were all on a level at Wolfson. The Chief arrived and I nervously offered him a drink. He was a gentleman and by the time Jack arrived we were getting along well. I have no doubt that it was another of Jack King's ploys to settle me into university life.

I had been at Wolfson for about three weeks when Jack called me into his office. 'Guest night soon Bill. You will need to invite your sponsor,' Jack announced.

'What, the Midland Bank?' I asked.

'No, Sir Philip Knights,' said Jack.

'Invite my Chief Constable? He probably won't know who I am,' I protested. 'He won't come here for me.'

'Nonsense,' said Jack. 'Here's the letter. Sign it.'

I did so, with no great hope of a positive response. I was wrong. A reply soon arrived. Sir Philip apologised for his non-availability, but said that he would send ACC John Glyn, who had nominated me.

The guest night was a grand affair: many courses; fine wines; two seating plans, one for dinner and one for dessert. We, as a Course, had laid on a bar in our 'house' for drinks before and after dinner. It was hugely enjoyable, all our guests had a splendid time and Mr Glyn was extremely good company. The only blight on the evening was that the students' level of alcoholic tolerance was higher than some of the guests', including Mr Glyn, who finished up slightly the worse for wear! I was confident that the visit had done my future no harm at all.

The course progressed and each week was more enjoyable than the last. A second guest night took place in Lent term and once again Jack produced a letter to Sir Philip for my signature. Sir Philip once again apologised for his non-availability but promised to send his deputy Ron Broome. I was progressing! I had never met Mr Broome until his arrival on the evening of the guest night.

'Now young man,' he said. 'Before we begin you will not get me drunk like John Glyn.'

I protested, 'Sir, Mr Glyn could have refused, I didn't hold his nose.'

The deputy laughed and said, 'Very well, I am here to learn, not get drunk. Before we meet anyone I want you to tell me about the course, the programme for this evening and who I will be meeting. I don't want you to disappear at any time in case I need to ask you something. Clear?'

'Yes, sir, very,' said I.

This is going to be a difficult evening I thought, but again I was wrong. Mr Broome was quite charming and a very interested and interesting guest. At the end of the evening he thanked me and said, 'I will tell the Chief that this is a very worthwhile course and that you are doing well.'

A success!

The term ended all too soon for me, but not for my

family as I found on my return home. There was a banner across the front of the house reading 'Welcome Home Bill', there were balloons and ribbon and the butcher opposite had given my wife some of his glass paint, and all the front windows were covered in messages. It was as though I had come back from the war!

I returned to duty in Special Branch and found it very difficult to settle. The job was very interesting, but I did not find it challenging enough and the left wing was very restrictive. The problem was soon to be resolved for I was transferred from Birmingham to run the satellite office at Coventry. Coventry was a problem as part of the West Midlands: whereas before it had sat nicely in the middle of Warwickshire, it was now part of the West Midlands. The city of Coventry was totally separate from Birmingham and the surrounding boroughs. Coventry people did not go to Birmingham and vice versa. Crime and related problems were therefore parochial and so it was with Special Branch.

I became responsible for the whole spectrum of Special Branch matters, not just the left wing. It was almost an autonomous posting and it was said that Mr McCaughey could not find his way to the Coventry office without a guide. I had some very good officers and one or two were quite exceptional in their specialist field. I still had the famous Geoff of Newquay fame but yet to come was his collision with the 'unlit, unattended, motorcar'.

They were happy times and it was from here that I was to be promoted.

I had applied for promotion to Chief Inspector on four occasions before being selected. On my first attempt I was not expected to succeed but went for the experience. The system was that all applicants would be interviewed by boards chaired by an ACC sitting with two Chief Superintendents. From this a list would be published for those selected for second interview and from this interview, the successful candidates would be selected.

I was pleased on my first attempt to make the second

stage and held high hopes for the following year as a large proportion of my fellow interviewees had been promoted and I thought there would be less competition. I once again reached the second stage and I thought that I was a 'cert'. Both my first and second attempts took place whilst I was at Tally Ho! and on the second occasion I was supported by my mentor David Gerty.

We knew that the results were imminent and one afternoon I was called out of class and there in the corridor was Mr Gerty. 'Bill, I'm sorry you've not been selected. I felt that I should tell you myself,' said the ACC.

I was disappointed, but this was tempered by the ACC having taken the trouble to come and tell me.

'Next year you should be OK. They think you need to go outside first,' Mr Gerty told me.

I thanked him and returned to my class. They were right, I was not yet ready but was convinced that I would be selected the following year. I had transferred to Special Branch and attended Wolfson prior to the next round of promotion boards. I had also been interviewed by Sir Philip Knights when my report arrived from Cambridge.

Sir Philip had told me that he had called me to discuss the report as Wolfson was a new venture. He asked me a great number of questions and then told me that there were two reports, one from Jack King and the other from my tutor. He said that they told him more about me than any other report or appraisal in my file. He told me that the reports would stand me in good stead in the future.

I was very confident when I was called for promotion board interview and prior to the first stage I met with an old Warwickshire colleague, Tom Baldwin, in my local. Tom was coming to the end of a Bramshill Scholarship which was a three-year degree course at Warwick University. As he had been away for over two years, he expected to be told to wait for a year before promotion. I was to follow Tom on the interview day at the same board.

I felt that I had performed well and saw it as a foregone

conclusion that I would reach the second stage, having done so on two previous occasions. I was stunned when the list came out. I had failed. Tom Baldwin was through! We were both surprised.

A week or so later, I got into the lift at Lloyd House. ACC John Glyn was in there.

'Hello Tom. How are you?' said Mr Glyn.

I didn't answer him of course.

'Tom,' said Mr Glyn looking at me, 'I asked how you were.'

'My name's Bill,' I said. 'You think I'm Tom Baldwin don't you?'

He denied it and I continued, 'You do. That's why he passed and I didn't – you got us mixed up.'

The lift doors opened and he got out without answering me.

I remained convinced that he had mixed us up – we were not dissimilar in appearance, the same age and similar backgrounds in Warwickshire. I became a somewhat difficult member of staff for a few weeks, but everything passes with time.

My successful board was in the spring of 1981. I was DI at Special Branch Coventry office. The boards had been completed and the results were awaited. My telephone rang.

'Hello Bill, it's David Gerty. You're through the boards to Chief Inspector. Well done.'

I was once again amazed: the ACC crime ringing personally to tell me of my success as he had done with my failure. What a gentleman! I thanked him profusely.

'That's not all,' he said. 'You are to be promoted to DCI next week and I'm putting you in charge of the Drug Squad.'

'But I don't know anything about drugs,' I said.

'I know, that's why you are going there. I want you to sort it out.'

Mr Gerty arranged an appointment with me to see him and ended the conversation.

The Drug Squad. I knew nothing about them, not even where they were based. I had no experience of drugs, either personally or professionally. This was to be a serious challenge.

I saw David Gerty who told me that he had serious concerns about how the Drug Squad was being run. It was not his intention to tell me how to do the job, but he did insist that the squad target and arrest dealers, not people in possession of minor amounts of drugs for personal use. He was looking for efficiency and an effective unit to combat drug misuse.

I was to be promoted and take over command of the Drug Squad in mid-May 1981 but before I could do so I was told that I had been selected to attend the Junior Command Course at the Police Staff College, Bramshill. There had been a reorganisation and restructuring of college courses and the Junior Command Course was for officers fitted for Chief Inspector rank. It was a six-month course! The course was to begin in June 1981 I was to be in post at the Drug Squad for two weeks before departing for Bramshill. Mr Gerty's reorganisation plans would have to wait!

Chapter Fifteen

Drug Squad and Bramshill

I thought that the two weeks would give me a chance to look at the working of the squad and make an initial assessment of the staff. The West Midlands Drug Squad was at that time the largest in the country with 36 officers. There were three main offices: Bournville, covering Birmingham and the Central Divisions; Coventry for Coventry and Solihull where there was a small satellite office; and Darlaston to cover the Western Divisions. There were DIs in charge of each of the three offices.

I arrived at Bournville Lane police station, where I was based, on a Monday morning. I immediately rang the Detective Chief Superintendent Operations in order to arrange an appointment. I was greeted with, 'Why aren't you here? You should report here on your first morning.'

I said, 'I'm sorry. I understood that you are a busy man and it's necessary to make an appointment.'

The reply was 'Get down here now!'

A wonderful start. I did not know the Chief Superintendent other than by reputation. He was a Birmingham city officer widely experienced and the head of a group of Birmingham city detectives of Welsh origin known as 'The Taffia'. I drove into the city centre to Police

Headquarters and went to the Chief Superintendent's office. I knocked and entered, no handshake, no greeting, other than, 'You know that I didn't want you, don't you?' said the DCS.

'But you don't know me,' I protested.

'That's right and I don't want to. I made my selection, but 7th floor said it had to be you. You are going to Bramshill in a fortnight. Don't do anything stupid before then.'

I was absolutely amazed to be treated in such a manner. I said, 'I'm not stupid and I don't intend to do anything other than look and listen.'

I was dismissed. I was sorely tempted to complain, but as I was going away for six months, I decided to keep my own counsel until I returned in December. An age away.

Once again I had to be equipped with uniform for the course. There was a great deal to do in a short time and it was soon Sunday afternoon and time to leave home. Again!

Bramshill House is a delightful place and I was looking forward to spending the summer in such wonderful surroundings. I knew that the Junior Command Course had replaced the Inspectors' course and presumed it would be much the same. I was certainly hoping for 'Language and Literature'. Rooms were allocated and syndicates assigned. My syndicate director was to be Superintendent Graham Ward from Derbyshire, who seemed very pleasant. Sunday nights are quiet at Bramshill, but there were a considerable number of us from West Midlands so we gathered in the bar.

Monday morning brought a number of surprises. The first was at breakfast when I bumped into Christine Gowland, my assessor from Ryton-on-Dunsmore. She was delighted to see me and felt reassured that she knew someone on the course. There were only two women on a course of over 150 men; difficult for them. The other woman to whom Christine introduced me was Pauline Clare, now Chief Constable of Lancashire and the first woman to hold such a post.

The second surprise was to find that my Academic Director was to be John Rhind, my old friend from 1976. I was at an advantage: I was on that first day the only Chief Inspector in my syndicate of 14, although this was to change during the course as others were promoted. It was also an advantage to have been there previously for four months. I thought that I would be able to avoid any difficult 'monitors' jobs' by volunteering for what I knew to be the less demanding roles. No such luck.

Graham Ward, our director, introduced himself as our 'facilitator'. He said our success would be judged on how little we bothered him: 'self teaching' was to be the thing.

'Idle bugger,' I wrote in my notebook.

He explained the course content and how the timetable was to work, how we would select our specialisms and the workload, how many essays in other words. Then he started to dish out the monitors' jobs. I volunteered for several but was ignored.

'Stage show,' said Mr Ward.

A rotten job and there were to be two stage shows, designed and presented by students on guest nights. The rep was expected to fully participate. A thankless task. I got it.

'Mr Hannis. I understand you are something of a comedian. You can do that,' said Mr Ward.

I thanked him. John Rhind had obviously spoken!

Graham Ward proved to be a pleasant and helpful director but did like to go missing whenever possible. I understood his reasoning. He was married to a statuesque former policewoman, they had a young baby and were living in a caravan on a site nearby. They were naturists and the caravan site was a nudist colony. This caused ribald comment and was also the cause of a hilarious incident.

In addition to his duties with us, Graham was responsible jointly with a member of the academic staff for a specialist subject. Ivor was Graham's academic and he invited him for tea at the caravan. Ivor was unaware of the naturist aspect of Graham's life and as they drove on to the site, he

135

was amazed to see naked men walking about.

'Look Graham, these men haven't got any clothes on,' said Ivor.

'Oh, didn't I tell you?' said Graham. 'This is a nudist colony.'

Ivor was stunned and even more so when they drove up to the caravan and Graham's wife appeared to greet her guest stark naked. Graham got out of the car and took his clothes off. Poor Ivor had to sit through tea with two naked people. He never forgave Graham!

The first stage show meeting was a revelation. Most of the other representatives were volunteers, not pressed men and were anxious to display their talents. All courses were represented and the Superintendents' Course took control. The pressed men were happy to take a back seat. By the time the third meeting came along, it was clear to me that the show would be a disaster, as the performers were deluded as to their talent. 'The Blood Donor' is hilarious with Tony Hancock but not with an Inspector in a dirty mac; 'Miss Joan Hunter Dunn' is a marvellous poem, but not when performed in a monotone.

I decided we needed some humour. I said that I would write and perform in a Monty Python-type sketch and that I would devise a funny opening for the show to set the tone (hopefully).

I wrote a sketch and called it 'Bramshill Wives'. It was two women talking in a launderette: they were the wives of two Bramshill students and discussed why their husbands never wrote home, phoned home, went home or invited them to a guest night. All the excuses that I had picked up in 1976 and the present course were included. I decided to dress the two women in dresses, trainers, hair nets and head-scarves, but the problem was to find someone to do it with me. I eventually persuaded Mike Rogers from Wiltshire to take the part.

When the night arrived of the first show we opened with John Game, a City of London officer walking to the grand

136

piano at the front of the main body of the assembly hall. He was in black tie and sat at the keyboard and began to play the first few bars of Tchaikovsky's Piano Concerto Number One in b Flat Minor which he could do very well – but that was all he knew, the first few bars. As he was playing a student came into the back of the hall and shouted, 'Mr Game, telephone call!' John stopped playing, stood up and walked out. We were convulsed, but the audience didn't know what was happening!

The programme began: 'Blood Donor' and 'Joan Hunter Dunn', together with other acts, were well received and then we were on! It was a hoot: the audience thought it was hilarious, or at least most of them – some were subject of direct attack and many were uncomfortable sitting with their wives to whom they had given the excuses we were now using. We were cheered off! It was such a success that we were asked to reprise it for the second show months later. We happily did so, using both the original material and additional material that I had written involving members of staff including Graham and his nudist activities. My role was to help temper some adverse remarks in my final report.

There were many other guest nights during the course which did not involve stage shows. Each was on a Thursday night when students were allowed to invite friends and loved ones. Numbers were restricted, each of the students' syndicates being allowed a number on each night. There was very little animosity in the syndicates and we all took our turns. The format was generally a reception arranged by several syndicates jointly for their guests before dinner and then after dinner, which was a formal affair, everyone adjourned to the bar. I had developed an interest in the history of the house during my 1976 course and my knowledge was such that I was able to conduct a decent tour of the house for guests. It soon became practice for those students whose guests were interested to put them on 'Bill's tour' before dinner – which resulted in many drinks for Bill after dinner!

137

I wanted Jack King from Wolfson to be a guest and he arranged a lift by ensuring that a Cambridgeshire student invited the Assistant Chief Constable, Bernard Hodson, who would be provided with a car and driver as it was classed as an official visit.

Jack was, and is, larger than life. He arrived early and began by saying, 'Take me to Newman, I have some books for him.'

I told Jack that Sir Kenneth Newman, the Commandant, held an invitation-only drinks reception before dinner and that I was not on the list. I told Jack that I would arrange a meeting after dinner (I hoped!).

I had a plan for Jack that evening, apart from drinks and dinner, and I did not want him to disappear.

I had become friendly during the course with a Sergeant Philip Wharton from the Metropolitan police. He was a member of the 'Special Course' which was part of an accelerated promotion scheme for exceptional officers with potential for the highest ranks. Many of the students on this course were graduates and those who were not, were eligible to apply for a Bramshill Scholarship, which gave leave of absence for three years to obtain a degree from a university. Philip had been awarded such a scholarship, but was unsure of where to make his application. Our friendship had stemmed from playing hockey for the college: he was a very swift forward, and I the goalkeeper, a position in which I had played for Warwickshire police and the West Midlands police for some fifteen years. I was well out of practice by 1981, but the games were enjoyable and the social aspect even more so. Philip was a very bright and personable young man and I said to him, 'Would you like to go to Cambridge?'

'Of course,' replied Philip, 'who wouldn't? But there's no chance of that.'

'I'll get you in,' I said airily.

I then told Philip about my Wolfson course and Jack King. I arranged Jack's visit and told Philip to be in the bar after dinner in the Prince of Wales room where I would arrange for him to see Jack. I am sure that he thought I was mad, but he agreed to do as I suggested.

After dinner on the guest night, we adjourned to the bar in the main house. Jack was suitably mellow, but still concerned about the books he had brought for 'Newman'. I decided to get this out of the way before bringing up the subject of Philip. I discovered that Sir Kenneth was holding court in the tapestry room on the first floor. I took Jack there and was about to introduce him when Jack thrust out his hand poked Sir Kenneth with his finger and said, 'Here are those books you wanted. I said I would bring them when I was next down.'

Sir Kenneth smiled and looked quizzically at me. Before I could speak, Jack was off again. 'King, Wolfson, we were at a lunch.'

'Ah, yes, how nice to see you again,' said Sir Kenneth.

Jack introduced me. 'You know Bill Hannis of course, one of your students and mine, excellent prospect.'

I grinned weakly. Eventually I managed to extricate Jack and took him to the bar. I armed him with a drink and took him to the Prince of Wales room. Philip was sitting in an armchair and I signalled with my eyes to remain where he was. I then explained to Jack about Philip, sang his praises and said that I thought he would make a fine mature undergraduate addition to both Wolfson and the university.

'Tell him to get in touch with me,' said Jack. 'I'll see what can be done.'

'He's sitting over there,' I said, pointing at Philip.

'Very well, bring him over,' Jack said, clearly a little put out at being trapped so easily. I introduced Philip to Jack who then said to me, 'Go away. Come back in half an hour with another drink.'

I left them to it.

I returned after about half an hour. Philip seemed at ease and Jack said

'Well, this is very unusual, but Bill is right, you will do

139

well at Wolfson. I will take you. Bill will tell you where to write, now let us get on with the evening.'

Philip left grinning broadly whilst Jack and I concluded a very convivial evening. Jack is in his element when he knows so many people, which he seemed to do wherever I saw him.

Jack was true to his word and Philip became a mature undergraduate. He was very successful both academically and as a full member of the university. He became Secretary of Wolfson College Amalgamated Club and a mainstay of Jack's 'police students'. I attended a number of dinners as Philip's guest in his three years. Sadly he is no longer a policeman having suffered a serious back injury whilst policing a demonstration.

The main purpose of the Police College was not social but professional. The course was intended to fit the students for their first independent command and this was therefore a very serious syllabus. 'Language and Literature' had gone, things were wholly more professional but still sometimes a bit woolly. There were a number of pseudo-academics masquerading as policemen and a number of academics who clearly would not 'hack it' in true academia. Nevertheless it was overall a rewarding experience.

My main concern on arrival was to find time to learn something about drugs. I learned on the first day that there were to be a number of essays during the course and that one was to be a 'major' essay of some eight thousand words. There was to be a consultative meeting between me and my two directors Graham Ward and John Rhind to discuss the subject of the essay. I told them that I was going to write on 'Drugs and their Criminal Use'. They were not happy as they wanted to choose the subject, but I was not having any argument.

I said, 'I am here to be fitted for my first command which is to be the largest Drug Squad in the United Kingdom. The Police Staff College is going to look pretty stupid if I go back to my force knowing no more about drugs than when I left and that is nil.'

140

They reluctantly agreed. The essay was an ongoing project throughout the course, there was a great deal of other work in addition to various shorter essays on other subjects. There were operational plans, building plans, major incident scenarios, all to be presented in written form, either individually or as group projects. There was still time however, for sport, badminton in my case, and pub visits. The major essay was subject to tutorial discussion. I was well pleased with my work and increased knowledge, but the time came for the final paper to be submitted: eight thousand plus words and all to be typed by me!

I attended my final drugs tutorial. Both Graham and John were pleased with the content, but critical of the presentation. 'There must be a hundred typing errors,' said John.

'There must be a nearer a thousand,' I said. 'I did it myself, I'm not a typist.'

'Why did you not get your office to type it?' said Graham.

I said, 'Well strangely enough, they are very busy with operational matters and would not thank me for ordering them to type this instead of a court file.'

Another black mark!

I had selected 'Community Policing' as my professional specialism. The syllabus was again wide-ranging with many interesting visiting speakers and a visit to St Paul's in Bristol. Our professional director was Brian Moseley, which he pronounced 'Mossley' rather than the 'Sir Oswald' version. His own special area was gypsies. He was very well known in Romany circles and was always invited on-site when there was an encampment established at the end of the drive at Bramshill. The academic was Norman Greenhill, known as 'far away'. Each student was given a subject to study on which we were to produce a three-thousand-word essay and make a fifty-minute presentation to our fellow students. No problem to me as a trained instructor, but very difficult for those unused to presentations.

I was given 'Homosexuality', which was not an easy subject, for even policemen get embarrassed when hearing in detail about sodomy and gross indecency as I knew from my experience at Tally Ho! The law was no problem to me as I had taught it for two years and I researched developments and practice in both the UK and the USA as a comparison. The fifty-minute presentation was to include an allowance of at least five minutes for questions. The practice was to plant three or four questions with fellow students in order to both fill the time and appear knowledgeable.

I did well, I used humour but covered the subject and kept interest. Question time came and my planted questions were well answered. The two directors always asked questions to ensure that you had really done your homework. All went well until Norman Greenhill said, 'Mr Hannis, what is the attitude of the Church of England to homosexuality in the clergy?'

I replied, 'At this time, it is considered desirable, but not yet compulsory.'

Great laughter from my colleagues, but both Brian Moseley and Norman Greenhill were outraged.

The time came for my tutorial at the end of the course. Mr Moseley said, 'Your essay and talk were the same, how do you account for that?'

'Because that is how I wrote them,' I replied.

He said, 'They should have been different.'

'That's ridiculous,' I said. 'How can you do two different papers on the same subject in the time given?'

Mr Moseley's response was, 'You don't take this seriously. I will be giving you an adverse report.'

Wonderful! I am really doing well!

I thought things might improve when I was selected to be seen by the Dean of Academic Studies, Ian Watt, a witty and charming man with a wonderful mellifluous voice. He saw some one in ten of the students to review their progress. I got on well with him when talking in the bar and looked forward to a positive interview.

142

'Ah, come in Mr Harris,' said the Dean when I arrived in his study.

I did not correct him as all my life I have been called Harris by people who think that I have mis-spelt my name. The Dean began to review the course and my involvement. He was complimentary and I was very pleased until he mentioned a subject which I was not studying.

I said, 'Whose file is that Mr Watt?'

'Why yours, of course, Mr Harris,' replied The Dean.

'But my name is Hannis,' I said.

Consternation from the Dean as it was CI Harris's file – nothing at all to do with me! The Dean did not want to see me at all!

A few weeks after returning to force, I was called for interview with Sir Philip Knights who always saw everyone returning from the Staff College. Sir Philip discussed the course in general and my new role at the Drug Squad. He turned to my report and asked me to explain the comment 'his humour is sometimes misplaced' by Brian Moseley. I told Sir Philip my story and he laughed and said that neither Mr Moseley or Mr Greenhill were noted for their humour. He then told me that the adverse comment was more than tempered by the comment from Graham Ward: 'He was the star of both stage shows.'

'You obviously know when to place it well,' said the Chief.

He congratulated me on a good report and said that he would watch with great interest how the Drug Squad progressed.

I now only needed to sort out the Drug Squad to fit myself for my next promotion to Superintendent.

Chapter Sixteen

The Drug Squad

There had been two important changes in Drug Squad personnel during my absence, with a new DI having been appointed at both central and western offices: Sandy Craig at Bournville and Sid Law at Darlaston. I had met Sandy as a DS on an advanced course at Tally Ho! I did not know Sid, but both were very experienced officers with no Drug Squad experience. This was ideal from my point of view as both were clean sheets of paper, not old ideas. Graham Drew, the DI at Coventry, was also very experienced, but a long time Drug Squad officer. He was well qualified to do my job and could have been resentful, but he was not, although he was very wary.

There were a number of immediate tasks: the assessment of the drug problem, the staff, the offices, relationships with Divisions and other agencies. Firstly, I had to stamp my authority by earning some respect and secondly it was essential to gel with the three DIs to ensure that we all worked as a team.

Friday at the end of my first working week provided an opportunity to earn respect by doing a 'Douglas Bader' that is 'flying the spitfire' as he did when appointed to the Canadian squadron. An anonymous letter arrived on that Friday addressed to me as 'Head of the Drug Squad'. It was obviously written by a distraught mother of a young drug addict. She believed that the dealers were the problem and identified a specific flat in a large multi-occupied house in

Moseley, Birmingham, as a source of drugs and in particular heroin. The letter gave details of signals for showing clients that heroin was available, which related to a display of plant pots in the window. The mother also wrote that early Friday evenings was a known dealing time.

Anonymous letters are notoriously dangerous but this rang true. I discussed the matter with Sandy Craig and instructed that enquiries be made to try and corroborate some of the details in the letter. I had already been preaching during the week about the need for good intelligence before obtaining a search warrant and had emphasised that a negative search warrant would require a personal explanation to me. I was therefore treading a dangerous course.

In early afternoon, Sandy came to see me with Jess Brown, an old-time Drug Squad DS. Jess said that the house details fitted the letter and that a known drug dealer lived there, but it was not known in which room.

I authorised application for a warrant and told Sandy to organise the raid. I said that I would go along as an observer in order to see how the team worked. I said that I would go in my own car as the address was on my way home. Famous last words!

The raid began a short time before 6pm, as the plants were in the window in the right pattern. The window was on the top floor. Sandy and his team went into the house and I waited outside telling Sandy to call me when he had gained entry and secured the premises. I had only been there a few minutes when a young man walked towards the front door. He nodded to me.

I said, 'Hi, are you going up to see ———?' naming the man who was known as a dealer.

He said, 'Yeah, I've got some gear for him.'

I said, 'You're nicked.'

I identified myself and cautioned him. He was speechless. I took hold of him and walked him into the hallway. I called Sandy and explained what had happened. We were both grinning broadly.

'OK gaffa, I'll take him upstairs,' said Sandy.

I said that I would wait outside.

A few minutes later another man in his twenties walked onto the forecourt of the house.

'Hello,' I said. 'Do you want ———?' smiling at him and thinking 'this is easy'!

He was off and running: I set off after him shouting the traditional, 'Stop! Police!'

He did not. Long experience had taught that a reasonably fit fugitive fuelled by adrenaline had wings on his heels. There was normally one chance to grab him and if that failed, it was a chase and a contest to see who tired first. That is exactly what happened this time. I made a grab for him and missed. I had just spent six months playing badminton, hockey and using the gym. I was fitter than I had been for years, but I could not catch him.

'You won't get away!' I shouted after him and kept pace.

I had no idea where we were but realised we were going in a circle. I suddenly noticed that he was opening packets and throwing white powder in the air. I was getting very breathless and then saw that we were back near the original house. I saw Sandy Craig outside the house. I could not speak, I made a noise and pointed at the fugitive who was on the other side of the road to Sandy. Sandy soon assessed the situation and as a former captain of Penecuick Rugby Club tackled the fugitive and held him. Other officers came out to see what was causing the commotion. I was trying to explain what had happened when Sandy said, 'Christ gaffa. Don't move – you're covered in heroin.'

I looked down and saw that my front was covered in white powder. I was hoovered down and as this was being done, I told Sandy that the fugitive had been dropped off by a man in a Jaguar car which was parked around the corner. Two officers were despatched and came back triumphant – they had arrested a wanted drug dealer in possession of heroin and a large amount of cash! I was the hero of the hour!

146

I told Sandy to carry on and sat on the wall for a rest. A car pulled up and another man got out.

'Is ——— in?' asked the man.

He was very surprised when I arrested him and sent for Sandy. Sandy said, 'Gaffa, go home. We can't handle any more.'

Douglas Bader would have been proud of me!

The team building of the DIs took a little longer. I began by arranging a full morning meeting to discuss strategy and in order to emphasise the four-working-as-one theme I put on a good buffet lunch in my office which I prepared myself. There was plenty of food and drink and a constructive meeting concluded with a very convivial lunch. This eating in the office adjacent to the central Drug Squad office also served as a signal to the troops that the leaders would be working together.

There had clearly been too much leeway allowed to the staff previously. This was not only illustrated by their work but also by their dress. Officers in their late thirties would appear in jeans with T-shirts carrying a large cannabis leaf design and similar drug-related logos. I asked one of the DCs why he dressed in such an outlandish manner.

'It's to blend in Sir, when we are working,' was the reply.

'Blend in where?' I asked.

'In pubs,' said the DC as though I were a child.

I asked 'Why? Are they fancy dress pubs?'

'Of course not, it's so that we don't stand out as police,' said the corpulent bearded figure.

'I see that. They wouldn't think that anyone so stupid could be in the police, would they?' I said to him.

He did not answer. I issued an order that normal dress would be smart casual with a suit, shirt and tie for court or other formal appearances. 'Dress down' would be for dirty jobs or undercover work such as observations. The lack of common sense was also apparent in delicate operational matters. I noticed a man with long hair and a large dangly earring in the main office and later in the police club. I asked who he was.

'That's ———,' was the reply.

'What does he do?' I asked.

'He's our best informant,' was the reply.

An informant in the office! In the police club! Good identity protection!

I made enquiries relating to this man and found that he was indeed very successful. I reminded the DIs of the need for security and the protection of the identity of our officers, offices and information. By his very nature, the man was an associate of our criminal targets and he had been given free access to our operational centre! I wondered if he was a double agent. Later events proved my fears to be well founded.

One area that ACC David Gerty had stressed to me on my appointment was the relationship with HM Customs and Excise Investigation Division. Mr Gerty was friendly with Vic Mitchell, the Assistant Chief Investigating Officer of the branch in Birmingham. He was responsible for all matters relating to drugs importation, VAT fraud and all other Excise duty evasion. There was a senior investigating officer in charge of each section and David Gerty had emphasised that I must form a good working relationship with the SIO responsible for drugs.

I made myself known to the SIO by telephone and first met him when a briefing was held at their offices in relation to an expected drugs purchase taking place in the West Midlands police area.

The Investigation Division were a group of intelligent, bright and highly-trained investigators. They had enormous powers and I thought very highly of them. There was, however, a bad feeling between them and the Drug Squad officers which stemmed from problems of corruption in the Metropolitan Police district in the 1970s.

The drugs SIO was David Ramsey, a very confident and well-spoken man. The briefing was for his officers, my officers and, I found on my arrival, the West Midlands Serious Crime Squad. I had no role in the operation and was there to observe and later talk with David Ramsey. I was soon astounded. The operation was as a result of Crime Squad information and it was their 'job' as they saw it. The drugs were being transported from London and were to be exchanged for money at the Corley Service area on the M6. The operational plan was shown and a full briefing of the participants took place. The Crime Squad were to be armed!

I could not, as usual, keep quiet. I pointed out that Corley services was in the Warwickshire Police area and that their Chief Constable would not take kindly to having armed officers running about on his patch.

'Don't worry. It's OK,' said the Detective Superintendent Serious Crime Squad.

I doubted it.

The briefing clearly showed that the importation of drugs had taken place some time before. It was my view that this was a police matter and not a Customs case. I was making notes to this effect and also made some disparaging notes relating to the men running the briefing. I was engrossed and did not notice that someone was looking over my shoulder! By the end of the briefing, I was furious. My authority as head of the Drug Squad was being usurped not only by the Customs and Excise but also by the Serious Crime Squad. This was my first joint operation and only the second week of my new role. As I rose from my seat DS Monty Walker said to me

'You ain't happy with this, are you gaffa? I think somebody had better look out. Well done.'

He smiled and I said, 'Don't read over my shoulder, you might find your name there.' But I smiled at him. Clever lad!

I could deal with the Crime Squad problem easily by ensuring that instructions were given that all drug matters were reported to me. I could not deal so easily with the Customs and Excise or 'Church of England' as I came to

149

call them. I decided to take immediate action. I said to David Ramsey, 'I want to talk to you, now.'

He took me into his office and I said, 'I am in charge of all drug related crime in the West Midlands. Your jurisdiction extends to importation and that means Birmingham Airport unless you have followed consignments from ports elsewhere. Should I find you carrying out operations other than importations, I will arrest whosoever is handling the drugs. The Serious Crime Squad will no longer be dealing with drug matters unless I request their assistance. We can either work together or against each other, but be assured that David Gerty will be made aware of any lack of co-operation.'

He was stunned. I walked out, taking my officers with me.

'My God, what have I done?' I thought when I got back to my office.

The telephone rang and David Ramsey said, 'Lunch tomorrow?'

We went for a four-hour lunch the following day and from that day on we enjoyed an excellent working relationship which continued when David moved to Luxembourg and was replaced by Tony Bregonzi. We both had problems early on in persuading our staff to share information, but in time both groups learned to trust each other and it was my proud boast that West Midlands Drug Squad and Birmingham Investigation Division had the best working relationship in the country. We had many successful operations in the almost three years that I was in charge of the Drug Squad.

One result of co-operation with the Customs and Excise was the development of 'drug buying' arrests. David Ramsey agreed that any potential purchase of drugs already imported could be handled by the Drug Squad. He did exercise his veto where an operation required the drugs to be allowed to 'run', that is that we allowed the drugs to pass from one criminal to another in order to arrest all members

150

of the team. David insisted that he alone could make a decision to 'run' drugs. The normal practice was to substitute the drugs with another substance in order to remove the risk of losing a large amount of illegal substances. I had no problems with that decision as this made the rules very clear.

There were a number of problems involved when contemplating a 'drugs buy'. There must be no question of 'agent provocateur' but there was no danger of this if a large amount of heroin, such as one kilo, or any dealing amount was involved. An innocent person could not acquire such an amount of illegal drugs. In order to control the situation, the buyer needed to be a police officer as we dare not trust an informant with either the money or the drugs. The buyer was, therefore, 'undercover', a very dangerous occupation requiring a very versatile and courageous officer. These were days of experimentation in undercover work and budgets were limited. In order to create an appearance of affluence with minimum outlay, good class hotels were used for meetings and where necessary the undercover officer was provided with a 'flash' car, usually borrowed. The final obstacle was getting authority to draw large amounts of cash from the bank. Some senior officers were more worried about losing the money than the safety of the undercover officer.

The normal routine was to have an informant effect an introduction between buyer and seller. Negotiations would include the production of a sample for testing to ensure quality and then arrangements for handover would be made. The venue for the handover needed to be containable without any officers being visible to the seller or his minders, who were normally present. The buyer needed to test the purchase before handing over the money, which would be the time for the arrest and this would have to take place before the seller realised that the full amount of money was not available. Senior officers were always reluctant to authorise the full amount but there was always sufficient for a good 'show' and to allow greed to over-shadow the natural caution of the seller. The undercover officer was always 'wired' either on his body, or if in a hotel in a fully 'bugged' room.

The first venture that I was involved in in my new role was at Brierley Hill. A garage owner involved in many illegal activities related to motor vehicles had decided to branch out into heroin. Everything had gone well, the buy was a kilo of heroin for £10,000, which was very cheap at that time. The operation was run by Sid Law, who was a very careful man who considered all eventualities. The exchange was to take place in the seller's garage premises, and we had agreed to this as it was easy to observe and contain. Sid had arranged for uniform backup including dog handlers. We had considered the firearms issue, but as there was no intelligence to suggest that the seller had any access to guns, we decided against it. No one liked having guns about unless it was absolutely essential.

On the evening of the buy, everything had proceeded well. The seller had a minder with him, but our man was alone. We could hear the conversation and everything went normally: the drugs were produced, the money was produced and the request from our man to chemically test the drugs was agreed. The test was positive, and the undercover officer said the key words which triggered the arrests. Doors burst open but as they did so, the minder reached inside his jacket and our man said, 'Christ, he's got a gun!'

A handgun was being produced when a dog handler let his dog go. The dog, trained to go for the gun arm, clearly got excited with all the noise and went straight for the groin. The minder dropped the gun and began to scream. The dog was called off and everything began to calm down.

A very successful operation: one kilo of heroin; one firearm; many stolen and forged vehicle registration documents and MOT certificates; and two prisoners – one with very sore testicles!

There were many similar successful operations during

152

my time with the squad. Some were combined operations with the Customs and Excise and others solely Drug Squad. There were a number of talented officers prepared to take on the undercover role and it was somewhat difficult to tell them their time was over. My own view was that they were only good for a maximum of three jobs as beyond that they would become known which was dangerous for all concerned. They were an unusual breed and could be difficult to control in a remote situation as they had to 'think on their feet' which could sometimes lead to problems.

One of our most successful buyers posed as a former rock musician, which he had been before joining the police. He was very convincing but for some reason decided to vary his story on one occasion. He told the buyer that he was a circus owner from East Anglia. We had provided him with a Triumph Stag and he adopted a large gold earring and a red spotted bandanna as a cravat. He was so convincing that the seller asked him for some circus tickets for his children!

The same officer was the buyer in what was the biggest cash buy during my time. The buy was for a large quantity of heroin for £90,000, a very large amount of money. Preliminary arrangements had gone well and it was now necessary to produce the cash. There was no way that I was going to be given authority to withdraw £90,000 and after much argument, it was agreed that I could have £30,000. The bank were somewhat reluctant even though it was the Police Authority money, and they asked us not to break the seals on the bundles of notes in order to make sure that they did not have to count it again. I thought that this was a minor problem, but agreed to their request.

The exchange was to be in a hotel. We had taken three adjoining rooms with the buyer in the middle room. We wired the room and put the £30,000 in one briefcase and filled the other with newspapers, as it was only intended to open the one case.

The planned day arrived, but there was a hiccup. The

sellers, two Asian men, postponed to the following day. The only problem with this was where to lodge the £30,000. The banks were closed and the Superintendent at Bournville Lane would not allow the money to be put in his safe as the insurance was limited to £5,000. I tried several other police stations, but was given the same answer. The only solution was to take it home! I spent a very unsettled night with £30,000 of uninsured money under my bed.

The following day, the operation went ahead as planned. There were two sellers and one buyer and three packets of heroin. It was necessary to test all three packets before making arrests and my officer was presented with a dilemma in how to prevent the sellers looking into the second brief case. His solution was simple. He had prepared by ripping all the seals from the banknotes and when it was time to test the heroin, he emptied the brief case of the thirty thousand pounds all over the floor and said, 'Count that you bastards, you've never seen so much money in your life!' They were still scrabbling about on the floor when we burst in to arrest them.

The bank were thrilled when I took the money back, all loose and uncounted. They asked me to stay and help, but I pleaded urgent duties.

I was very wary of the West Midlands Serious Crime Squad, not only because of the Customs and Excise example, but I felt that they were in some ways a 'necessary evil'. They were a very effective force against organised violent crime, and their officers were talented and brave, but they were something of a law unto themselves. Their highly-publicised downfall, when it came, was due to their failure to acknowledge change rather than any corruption.

They made contact with me one evening to say that they had information that a large amount of cocaine had been imported through Birmingham Airport and was at present in a house in Solihull. Immediate action was required. I happened to be at a social function with Customs and Excise and I explained the situation to the SIO and asked him to accompany me to meet with the Serious Crime Squad. We each took one of our officers with us. We listened to the story and asked questions. The 'importer' was well known, but the address given was not. The electoral roll showed a probable three generations living at the address, none of whom were known. There were only two choices: ignore the information or search the premises. The Serious Crime Squad were looking to me to supply a search warrant but I was very twitchy about the whole thing. I did not like to authorise applications for warrants on such information with no provenance of note and – even more importantly – there had recently been two highly-publicised negative searches of 'wrong' houses and one armed raid by the Serious Crime Squad.

I persuaded the SIO that with the urgency of the situation and the fact that this was an importation we should use the Customs and Excise 'Writ of Assistance', a very powerful, carefully-used document demanding assistance in the name of Her Majesty! Tony reluctantly agreed and we all proceeded to Solihull, via the Customs office to collect the 'Writ' from the safe.

We made a quiet approach to the house which was a large, detached residence in an affluent area of Solihull. I was not happy. There were no lights showing and it was by now very late evening. The SCS were all for putting the door in, but I instructed that we seek a uniform presence and whilst waiting I went to the neighbours. The occupant was a doctor and I acquainted him and his wife with what we were going to do and asked about the neighbours. He said that as far as he was aware, the only occupant was an old lady who was deaf, the main family being on holiday. The SCS were, however, adamant that their informant had pointed out the right house.

Tony and I decided to go in, taking the doctor with us, who turned out to be absolutely right – one occupant, a deaf old lady! Wonderful! We had forced the kitchen door as the lady could not hear us knocking. There was no cocaine! There

155

was in the grandson's bedroom herbal cannabis and reefer ends in a bedside table drawer. I would have been very suspicious had it not been one of my own officers that found it.

Tony Bregonzi was not best pleased, and neither were the neighbours who appeared in considerable numbers. I calmed everything down and we all went home.

I knew that the roof would fall in the next morning and arrived early at the office. I rang the Detective Chief Superintendent as soon as possible and explained the situation to him. He was a fan of the SCS and was happy to cling to a Customs Operation gone wrong rather than a third disaster for the West Midlands police. The media were not so easy to please and banner headlines ensued that evening. No mention of the Customs, only West Midlands police and the Drug Squad. Sir Philip Knights was not happy but accepted that I had acted in good faith.

Relying on the 'seven day wonder rule', I resumed normal work expecting another story to remove mine from the headlines, as it did within two days. My relief was short-lived.

One of my tasks as head of the Drug Squad was to give talks on drugs to various bodies. I enjoyed the role and was developing something of a reputation as 'good value'. I was not surprised, therefore, when, within three days of the Solihull debacle, I received a telephone call from a man identifying himself as an official of Solihull Rotary club. 'I understand you do a good talk,' he said.

'People are kind enough to say so,' I replied modestly.

'Our speaker has let us down and we need someone for tonight. Can you do it?' he continued.

'How did you get my name?' I asked.

'Sir Philip Knights said you would come,' said my caller.

'Uh-oh,' I thought. 'A set-up.' I agreed to attend.

I decided to arrive late so that I could not be button-holed before the dinner. I needed to survey the audience before speaking. Sure enough, there sat the doctor neighbour and two other neighbours from the abortive raid! Sir Philip had engineered a public examination! My dinner went down in lumps and I drank little. Eventually I was introduced and I went into attack mode.

'I think before my talk it may be of interest to some of you to hear my explanation for the badly-handled raid the other evening.'

I gave them a sanitised version of events and ended by saying that I understood their concern, but any complaint must come from the householder and whilst I could not give details the search was not negative! There were some questions on procedure and I then gave them my usual drugs talk. I felt it was well received.

Some days later I saw the Chief Constable. 'The residents of Solihull were satisfied Mr Hannis. Accountability is the key, let them see we have nothing to hide. Well done!' said the Chief.

'It's you that did well, Sir,' I thought.

One day I received a telephone call from my old friend Dr Ben Davies, the Home Office Pathologist. 'William, we are having a day on drugs at the Birmingham medical school. It's a meeting for former students. Can you oblige?' asked the Doc. I readily agreed and Dr Ben told me that it was a Saturday and I would be required to speak for an hour which included time for questions. I asked him to confirm and thought little more about it; my usual fifty minutes plus questions would be more than enough. I had by now honed my talk – it was informative, interesting, funny and controversial, or so I had been told on a number of occasions.

Dr Ben's letter informed me that I was the first speaker and I would be welcome to stay for lunch. I arrived full of confidence at Birmingham University and was directed to a large lecture theatre. I was greeted by the conference secretary.

'Can I have a copy of your paper Mr Hannis?' he asked.
'Paper, what paper?' I said.

'The paper you are giving to conference,' said the secretary.

'I haven't got a paper, I just give a talk,' I protested.

I asked for a programme and with a sinking heart I opened it. The speakers: me, Margaret Pereira, the head of the Forensic Science Service, a Police Surgeon and a High Court Judge!

'How many coming?' I asked, with some dismay.

'Two hundred plus. A good turn-out,' said the secretary.

I agreed and thought that what I had taken to be a few doctors having a nice lunch and a talk, was a major meeting on an important subject. Paper! I did not even use notes.

I was introduced and began, no paper, no notes, but I could talk and I knew my subject. I could soon tell that I had them with me and at the end there were many questions which I dealt with easily. The secretary rose to thank me and was very complimentary. He said that both he and the audience were amazed that I was able to speak for so long without notes. Thank you Harrogate!

There was a break before the next speaker during which the secretary asked me where he should send the transcript of my address for checking before publication! I left him in no doubt that all views were personal and not those of Sir Philip Knights and that neither he nor I would be pleased to see them in print!

The Drug Squad gave me many opportunities and a major one arose through my Wolfson connection with Ron Broome the DCC, who had been my guest. He never forgot me after his visit and my first indication of that was when he was addressing a major briefing for a force-wide operation. I and my team were late arriving and as we crept in at the back of the room, he said, 'We may now begin. The Thomas Hardy squad has arrived.'

I was quite pleased at the recognition and also that only he and I knew what he was talking about. Whenever I saw him thereafter he always had a kind word and would mention something to do with Hardy such as Roman

Polanski's film of *Tess*, much to the mystification of his colleagues. Mr Broome was promoted to Chief Constable of Avon and Somerset and one day he telephoned.

'Bill, I am to chair an ACPO [Association of Chief Police Officers] working party on drug-related crime. I want you to sit on it with me. I will square it with Sir Philip, if you agree.'

I readily agreed and regularly travelled to Kings Weston at Bristol to participate in the working party. It was a very successful report produced by a combination of high-flying ACPO members and pragmatic practical detectives. The report became the basis for legislation on seizure of assets obtained through drug trafficking.

This high profile work together with my growing reputation in the drugs field led to an offer to take up a post at what was then the Central Drugs and Illegal Immigration Intelligence Unit (CDIIIU) at Scotland Yard. This was a national unit and growing in reputation. It was a very tempting offer, but was for three years in the rank of temporary Superintendent. Very attractive, but three years was a long time, especially for my wife as I would be away from the force. I decided to invite myself for lunch at Wolfson College and seek Jack King's advice.

Following the usual excellent lunch, I told Jack of my problem.

'Excellent job, but too long. Two years is right. With two years, you are always coming back next year. Three years and it's, "Who?"' Very succinct.

'We'll ring Newman and see if we can get it down to two,' said Jack.

'You can't do that,' I said.

Too late, he was already ringing Scotland Yard. He asked for Sir Kenneth and was put through to his staff officer, another ex-student of Jack's and later to be deputy commissioner of the City of London police. The result was that the three years could not be changed. We decided to refuse the appointment.

The long-haired informant with the earring had been a very useful asset to the squad and was now under much better control. He now met his handlers away from the police station! I had seen him a number of times both to test his information and to emphasise the need for his non-involvement. He was very close to the drug scene at top level and we had to be very careful not to expose him. His handlers reported that he had been asked to participate in a large importation of cocaine from Spain via Dover. The plan was for a number of expensive sports cars to leave the country together and travel to Spain where one would have the cocaine concealed in the body of the car. Our man's part in the operation was to meet with the teams in Dover and to travel with them. He was not to import the cocaine.

Enquiries were begun and it was clear as to who the prime mover would be. Surveillance was arranged on his property, both physical and technical. We only confirmed his associates and our informant's connection and we therefore became reliant on the informant. We discussed the whole case with Customs and Excise at every stage. It was agreed that the informant could participate and that Customs would take over when the team returned to England. The informant was to keep us informed as much as possible without jeopardising his safety.

The informant was not informed of our surveillance or our operational plans. He was understandably nervous and we agreed to shadow him at a safe distance as far as departure from England in order that he could contact us in an emergency.

I decided that due to the nature of the operation, I would participate and naturally take command. We had arranged for the informant to use a Mercedes Cabriolet in order to fit in with the rest of the team. We agreed a time of departure, route and ETA for Dover.

We were driving down the M1 and were approaching the outskirts of London when I was required to contact my office by telephone. I was told that the informant had been arrested in possession of cannabis and was in custody at a

Metropolitan Police Station. He had given my name as a reference and I was required to attend forthwith!

I arrived at the police station with my two officers and was told that the arrest had been made by two traffic officers on the M1. The informant had passed their marked police car at 100mph. It was raining and our man had the car top down! The officers stopped him and he immediately said, 'I'm on a drugs operation for West Midlands, DCI Bill Hannis is running it. I'm taking these spliffs down to Dover for some dealers.'

He then produced a number of cannabis cigarettes, or spliffs. He was immediately arrested.

I asked to see my man, but this was refused. I first had to give an explanation to the local DCI. I told him the story and said that it seemed that my man had deliberately had himself arrested to avoid continuing with the operation. The DCI agreed that I could see the informant who could not give me a satisfactory explanation for his conduct. I was certain that the planned trip was genuine and probably bigger than we had been told. I was anxious to identify the participants and their vehicles and the only way to do this was to let the informant 'run'. I asked him whether he was prepared to continue on the understanding that he may still be prosecuted for possession of cannabis and that he did not travel with the team from Dover to the Continent. I said that we would remain close by and he agreed.

I then had to persuade the Met to release him, which they reluctantly agreed to do after talking to CDIIIU. We continued on to Dover and saw our man to his hotel. We were able to identify the team and their vehicles, but could also see that our informant was well settled in their company. The group were to travel the next morning, which meant that we had to spend a very chilly night in the car!

The informant did not come out of the hotel in the night as he had promised. I was concerned that he would travel and we could no longer trust him. I decided to prevent his departure by immobilising his car, knowing that he would not leave it in a car park for a week or more.

The following morning, our man was left in the car park trying to start his car. When he had been alone for some time, we went to him and returned his rotor arm! I castigated him for failing to follow instructions and told him that we would be in touch with him. We ensured that he drove beyond London before leaving him to his own devices.

We maintained the surveillance and were soon informed by Customs that the main suspect was at Dover in his Porsche. A full search was being made of the vehicle and eventually the car was virtually taken apart. There was no trace of drugs. We were very disappointed.

I decided to await the suspect's return to his home, hoping to see or hear something to our advantage. Sandy Craig and I waited in the observation point and very late in the evening the suspect arrived. He made a telephone call, but due to the system at that time, we were unable to get a verbatim report from the intercept. Shortly after the call, two other men arrived at the premises and there were scenes of great joy as though they had won a very important football match. We had clearly been thwarted.

The technical surveillance revealed that the importation had taken place, but it did not give any indication of the location of the cocaine. The surveillance also cast further suspicion on the informant's involvement. I became sure that the whole thing had been a sophisticated 'sting' to divert attention from the real importation. There was no proof however, and no action that could be taken other than to sever any working contact with the informant. I issued a written instruction that no Drug Squad officer was to have any dealings with our informant other than to arrest if necessary.

The matter did not end there. The MPD were clearly unhappy with the events of the afternoon and reported the matter to their complaints department who in turn passed the enquiry to the CDIIIU and the West Midlands Police. I had an uncomfortable few weeks before being cleared of any charge of misconduct.

My written instruction was ignored by an officer who was seconded from me to a major fraud enquiry. I recalled him and formally warned him, taking the unprecedented step, for me, of making a full pocket-book entry of our meeting. I was very pleased that I had made the entry when some weeks later the same officer was arrested in an under-cover operation involving the proposed importation of heroin. He was eventually found not guilty, but the fallout was considerable. I had ensured my non-involvement with my pocket-book entry.

A most unusual task came my way due to a tragic event. DI Sid Law had been in contact with police officers in Denmark through the CDIIIU in relation to the activities of a Black Country man in Nestved. He was involved in the importation and distribution of drugs both in Denmark and England, but the Danish police had been unable to catch him in possession. The man's wife was living in the West Midlands. The powers of the Danish police were such that they could tap telephones at the drop of a hat. They had listening devices on private and public telephones that the man was using, but they were not certain that they had covered all eventualities. The Danish police requested that we tap the wife's telephone in the West Midlands. The regulations here were very strict, requiring the Home Secretary's approval and he would not consider a telephone request from Denmark as sufficient grounds. It was eventu-ally agreed that Sid Law would travel to Denmark to look at the evidence first hand. The Danish police were also in great difficulty in understanding the Black Country accent and hoped that Sid would 'translate' the accent into under-standable English. They had asked Sid on several occasions whether the wife lived near a canal as it was often mentioned. They also asked what a 'tinrun down' was. Sid was unable to help with either question and clearly needed to hear the tapes first hand.

A 'Commission Rogotoire' was obtained in order to allow Sid to act as a police officer in Denmark and the travel arrangements were made. Sadly, two days before departure, Sid's father died. A quick replacement was needed and as I knew the facts, I decided to pull rank and go myself.

There were two firsts for me despite my age. I had never flown in a jet and had never been abroad. All family holidays had been in Great Britain and I had not flown since leaving the ATC, and that was only once in an aged Anson. I was to fly from Birmingham to Copenhagen where I was to be met and driven to Nestved.

Disaster! My ears went during descent. I could not hear a thing and I was there to listen to tape recordings! I was met by two officers to whom I explained my problem. They assured me it would pass and that I would be hearing normally the next day when work began. I was a real tourist on the way to Nestved and when I saw a road sign for Elsinor and said 'Hamlet's Castle', they smiled indulgently and explained that we were going to the other end of the island. I settled into my hotel and had a convivial evening but awoke the next morning still deaf. I was picked up and taken to meet the senior officer with whom I would be working. I was useless, and a doctor had to be found who could see me immediately. He kindly syringed my ears, for a fee of course. I returned ready for the fray.

I was taken to the room where they kept banks of tape recorders and this was only a small market town! The secretary knew exactly where the problem areas were on the tapes and we settled down to listen. I soon solved the problem of canals and the meaning of 'tinrun down'. There was a conversation between Denmark and a man in the Black Country. The Danish target was telling his friend how they had been returning from a drugs sale and had a large amount of cash and cannabis in their car. The police had tried to flag them down on the motorway and a chase had ensued. They had evaded the police and had buried the case with money and cannabis at 'the bottom of a telegraph pole with a piece of tin running down it'. ''Kin'ell,' said

164

his friend – 'Fucking Hell' being his response to most revelations!

The tapes took some two days to evaluate and a great deal of useful information was obtained. I wrote a short glossary of slang for the secretary and arranged for a more comprehensive version to be sent on my return. There was clearly enough evidence to authorise a warrant for a telephone interception at the wife's address and the visit was undoubtedly a success.

I was left with a free day on the Thursday as my return flight was Friday. At 9am on the Thursday a marked police car arrived at the hotel with a driver in civilian clothes: the same driver we had had during the week. The senior detective who came along to the hotel told me that provided I paid for the driver's meals the car was at my disposal and I was to be taken to Elsinor and then to Copenhagen for a tour of the city and finish at Tivoli for dinner. It was a delightful day which is still vivid in my memory.

The telephone intercepts, both at home and away, were very productive. They led to the arrest of a number of people including the main target in Denmark. They were caught in the act of transporting cannabis and cocaine into Denmark having travelled from Spain. I hope that he said ''Kin'ell' when he was arrested!

I had succeeded in the task set me by David Gerty in that the Drug Squad was an efficient unit, targeting drug dealers and working effectively with Customs and Excise. I felt able to apply with some confidence for promotion to the rank of Superintendent. Although only one rank higher that Chief Inspector, the gap in salary and responsibility was considerable. The rank was much sought after but the ratio of CI's to Superintendents was about three or four to one and vacancies were few. There were only a handful of Chief Superintendents in the Force and most vacancies came through retirements rather than through promotion. The salary difference in 1984 was £5,000 – a big jump that made a huge difference to pension as well as salary. The selection procedure was simple: applications were reduced to a short list interviewed by a board chaired by the Chief Constable sitting with his Deputy and an ACC. The first hurdle was to get on the short list and to do this I needed the recommendation of my Detective Chief Superintendent, the officer who did not want me when I was promoted. He had over the intervening period become more friendly but I was not sure of his support. I applied and awaited developments.

At the time of my application the DCS had decided to retire. As part of the farewell ritual he visited each station to buy his DIs and DCIs a drink. On the day of his visit to Bournville Lane I went along and happily accepted a drink from him. During the evening he made a point of talking to me. 'Well Bill, I know that I didn't want you, but I have to admit that I was wrong. You've done a good job,' said my leader.

I was very pleased and admired him for saying what he did and I thanked him.

'To make up for it, I've got you promoted,' he said with a smile.

'You mean that you've recommended me?' I said returning his smile.

'Same thing. You'll walk it.'

I thanked him again and bought him a drink.

I made the short list and awaited the interview. Preparation was difficult as you needed to rely on the common sense of the board to ask sensible questions and not deal in obscurities. I felt that I had prepared well and on the day of my interview I was in headquarters and bumped into a colleague who had appeared the previous day.

'How did it go?' I asked.

'OK, I think,' was the reply.

'Anything difficult?' I ventured, hoping for a clue from my rival.

'Not really, but as I thought the Police and Criminal Evidence Act came up.'

'Of course, what aspect?' I asked innocently. 'Training implications. I said it was the biggest challenge,' said my colleague.

'Chief Constable down,' I said airily, thinking that I had better have another look at that.

Sure enough one of the first questions from the DCC was. 'What is the greatest implication of the introduction of the Police and Criminal Evidence Act?'

I was able to give a comprehensive answer, thanks to my chance meeting. I felt it was going well until the Chief asked, 'Mr Hannis, what are the three greatest threats to policing in the next ten years?'

I said quickly, 'Heroin, disenchanted black youth and firearms.'

The Chief said, 'Mr Hannis, you have been on the Drug Squad too long.'

I felt less confident and hoped that he did not mean a transfer rather than promotion.

There was no set day for results. The process finished and we all knew that there was then a review before any announcement. I was at home on a week's leave and dressing for a day out with my wife when the telephone rang in the bedroom. My wife answered and handed it to me, 'Tom Meffen, Bill.'

Tom was the new ACC Crime who had taken over from David Gerty,

'You are through the boards. You'll be promoted to Superintendent next week.'

I was elated as he continued, 'Do you want to know where you are going?'

'Please,' I said.

'F1,' said the ACC.

'F1? Where's that?'

'Steel House Lane.'

'What, as Detective Superintendent?' I asked incredulously.

'No, uniform. Well done.'

167

Chapter Seventeen

Steel House Lane

Uniform Superintendent at Steel House Lane, the police station covering Birmingham city centre. I could not believe it at first, but when I thought about it I realised that Barry Kirton, my old DI from the Crime Squad was Chief Superintendent of the F Division. I suspected a plot.

I rang Barry the next day. 'You'll never guess where I'm going,' I said.

'I know and you'll be the last nail in the Brums' coffin when you get here. Just think, Birmingham run by two "County Wankers".'

I realised then that this was to be no easy posting: it was definitely not a 'Bobby's Job'.

I knew very little of Steel House Lane police station and arranged to see Joe Frost from whom I was to take over. I went to Steel House Lane and was taken up to the Superintendent's office where I was greeted by Joe and spent some considerable time with him. There was no time for a period in tandem and this briefing was to be all I was to get. I learned that in addition to Steel House Lane I had a police station in Newtown at Bridge Street West, a large canteen serving the Magistrates and Crown Courts staff and that the Central Lock-up adjoined the police station. The station was unique in that each uniform shift had two Inspectors. One in and one out. This was historical due to the demands of the enquiry desk and custody requirements.

Joe said that the paperwork generated was enormous, there was a substantial CID, a Shoplifting Squad, Traffic Wardens and myriad small groups catering for the unique demands of the centre of the United Kingdom's second city.

I left Joe's office to be introduced to my Chief Inspector, Pip Postans, a legend in Birmingham and he greeted me with the words, 'Welcome, you're my fifth.'

In other words he did not expect me to make a lot of difference. My secretary then said, 'And you're my tenth.'

I went home wondering what I was in for.

The new role developed into the most challenging and demanding of my service to date. The hours were long and the tasks so varied as to warrant a book on their own. I certainly felt when I moved on that nothing could provide a problem that I would not be able to deal with. There were demonstrations, riots, woundings, murders, major traffic problems, security scares and personnel problems of every possible nature. There were football supporters every Saturday of the season, and mass shop lifting, known as 'steaming'. In short, every day was like an examination question and it was all topped off by having the most demanding Chief Superintendent in the force in the considerable shape of Barry Kirton.

A few examples will illustrate the range of tasks and the inherent difficulties.

The miners' strike was in full spate when I took command of the sub-division and we had to provide personnel for national demands. The provision depleted normal strength and caused problems for the officers taking part as it was stressful both mentally and physically for those involved. Until one Monday morning the problems were far away from Birmingham city centre. On the particular Monday, I walked into the station at 8.30am following a few days' leave. I was carrying some clean shirts and newly pressed trousers on hangers as it was always essential to be well turned out. The office Sergeant greeted me with the words, 'No time to put those away, Sir. The miners have occupied Price Waterhouse.'

I learned that a contingent of South Wales miners had gained entrance to the offices of Price Waterhouse and occupied them. The situation was contained, but attracting much attention as the city began work.

I went to my office and saw Pip Postans putting on his uniform jacket. 'Morning, Sir. The miners are in Price Waterhouse, I'm just going to sort the buggers out,' said my deputy.

Just what was needed, Pip using his subtle methods!

'No you don't. I'm going. You stay here and look after things.' He was disappointed, but did not argue.

When I arrived at the office block, I found that they had occupied the 8th floor. The block was situated near Snow Hill and there were a large number of miners in the street cheering on their colleagues who were leaning out of windows and shouting. The Duty Inspector had the building well contained and I went to the occupied floor. Two senior partners of Price Waterhouse met me and explained that they did not want any force used, but that they wanted the miners out. Difficult. I spoke to the leader of the occupants through a door, as I could not persuade him to open it. Price Waterhouse were classed as the enemy by the miners due to their associations with the Coal Board. The demands were ludicrous and unobtainable, but I played for time. I ascertained that there was no food in the office, but that there was water. A siege began. Nothing allowed in and no concessions.

I was in constant touch with Steel House Lane by radio and received much advice but no interference from my Chief Superintendent. My authority was in no way usurped for which I was extremely grateful. The problem was mine and I knew that it could not be allowed to continue too long. It was a gift for the media.

In my talks to the occupying miners, I stressed the lack of food, hoping for a reaction. I got one. I was called to the street and saw a cardboard box being tied to a rope. The rope was hanging from the occupied offices and the box contained fish and chips, for it was now lunchtime. The outside contingent of miners were cheering and I decided that if I ordered a snatch of the box, we would have serious disorder as the adjacent Old Contemptibles public house was doing a roaring trade with the outside contingent. I let the box go up, much to the dismay of my seniors when they heard of it!

I gave instruction that no more food was to be allowed up and went back into the building. I then began some serious negotiating as I was very concerned that when the pub closed, the outside demonstrators would become a serious problem and provide the media with a field day. My line was simple: 'You are getting no more food, no demands will be met. You have good publicity and if you come out before the pubs close, you can celebrate a victory and no one will be hurt.'

I felt that I was getting somewhere, but time was running out and I decided to tell the occupants that I would guarantee no arrests and that Price Waterhouse would not proceed against the occupants providing there was no serious damage and no public disorder.

My final offer which ended the siege was that if they came out before the pubs closed at 2.30pm (it was now 2.15) I would arrange for the Old Contemptibles to stay open for an extra hour so that they could get a drink before departing for Wales. The Licensee readily accepted my extension of hours when I told him that I would keep a substantial police presence in the area and assist him to clear the pub at 3.30pm.

The miners came out of the offices at 2.25pm. It was a close call and I felt an excellent result. Barry Kirton congratulated me when I returned to the police station and then handed me the telephone. It was the DCC, Les Sharpe. 'Well done Bill, we were getting a bit worried when we saw the chips go up, but it was an excellent result.'

I thanked him and asked what he meant about the chips. He told me that I had been under observation all morning from the 7th floor of police headquarters which had a direct view of the whole incident! The whole of the Chief Officers had at some time during the morning viewed my efforts through binoculars. I had never thought about the location and was very glad that I was ignorant of the 'observations'.

There were regular security alerts of both specific and general nature relating to Irish terrorist activities. The former were always treated with great respect due to the history of IRA activity in bombing various city premises. There were also regular nuisance calls of bomb warnings that caused great disruption. We all learned quickly and there was one particularly busy day when one of my new Inspectors, Mick Tubb, said to me at the end of the day, 'I had never dealt with a bomb scare until today, but after twelve I think I'm beginning to cope.'

One morning a suspect car was parked in New Street, the heart of the shopping area. It was 8.30am and could not have been at a worse time. Army bomb disposal had been called and the city centre was virtually closed. Traffic was in chaos. I felt that the cordon was adequate and allowed some traffic flow, but I was wrong. The Army Captain said, 'Simple rule Superintendent. Never mind yardage – if you can see the bomb, it can see you.'

I preached that phrase thereafter.

The general alerts related to the threat level and at a certain level we were required to put physical measures into operation. For Steel House Lane this required one Constable on the main door and one patrolling the street outside. It was boring duty and natural therefore that the Duty Inspectors did not select their best officers for this irksome task. This led to problems from time to time, one of which could have been more embarrassing than it turned out to be.

One afternoon, an officer was patrolling Steel House Lane when he was approached by a woman. She was agitated and had blood on her clothing. She told the officer that she had just been discharged from the General Hospital which was on the opposite side of the road. She went on to say that she had murdered her flatmate and wanted to give herself up! The officer asked her where the body was and she gave him an address in Stechford. He said, 'That's not on us, you'll have to go to Bromford Lane.'

The woman left and the officer told no-one.

I knew nothing of this until I received a telephone call from my opposite number at Bromford Lane, who took huge delight in telling me the story which he ended by telling me that the woman had caught a bus to Stechford and reported the matter at his police station. They had detained her and on visiting the address given had found the body of a female, dead from head injuries! He thanked me, laughingly, and made it plain that he would be dining out on the story for months!

I was furious and stormed downstairs to the Control Room. I demanded to know who was involved and why I had not been told, for I could tell that it was clearly general knowledge at Control Room level. The Duty Inspector calmed me down and said that as they knew what my reaction would be they were trying to establish all the facts before informing me. I saw the officer concerned with his Inspector and told him calmly that he would be disciplined for neglect of duty at the conclusion of the inquiry. He was downcast and repentant and I dismissed him. Later I was in the police club for a drink before going home. I was with Pip Postans and saw the officer concerned in the incident laughing with colleagues; it appeared to me he was regaling them with the story. I went towards him and clearly the look on my face indicated that I was not thinking rationally for Pip said, holding me by the arm, 'Don't hit him Sir, you'll get the sack. He's not worth it.'

I said, 'Just get him out of here.'

The officer was removed from the club and normality resumed.

I was not happy with security from then on and made a point of keeping officers on their toes. One day I had been out and came into the station in full uniform. The inside security Constable was sitting on a chair inside the door reading a paperback. He looked at me and smiled as I came in.

'Stand up when I come in and concentrate on your job, and don't sit there reading bloody stupid books. What is it anyway?'

'It's the Bible, Sir,' said the officer.

Oh dear! 'Well stay alert,' I said, feeling about a foot high!

Events in the city centre were not only in the public eye, but in the eye of headquarters, as the Price Waterhouse incident showed. Minor matters became magnified and major matters became media events. There was a need for a guard against over-reaction and therefore over-policing, but one event caused us to throw caution to the winds.

A 'Stop the City' demonstration had been arranged and the experiences of the City of London had shown that there was a potential for serious disruption, damage and disorder. Barry Kirton produced a plan that involved two phases, one to police the routes into the city to discourage demonstrators from attending and also to remove any weapon or article of offence from their possession and the second to have the ability to swamp any disorder with police to prevent escalation. The first element used the Force Tactical Support Unit and the second aid from all Divisions of the force. The plan was complex and part of it was to sectorise the city centre by colour in order to simplify allocation of our uniform support. The colours – blue, red, green, etc. – needed to be put onto a large number of maps, as this was in the days before colour copiers. One evening therefore, a Chief Superintendent and three Superintendents were colouring maps by hand, each of us issued with a different coloured pen! I could not take this seriously and was roundly castigated when I suggested issuing colouring books to the Intermediate Command Course students at the Police Staff College to ready them for Command!

The great day arrived, but the success of phase one could not be predicted and the Divisional Aid plan had to be introduced. This involved 1-10s, that was one Sergeant and ten PCs arriving at intervals by personnel carrier from all Divisions. David Blick, the Superintendent at Digbeth, the other main Birmingham police station, and I were responsible for this phase. We had provided parking facilities in Steel House Lane for the vans. The day went very well, phase one worked brilliantly and there were far fewer demonstrators than expected. Those that did arrive were subdued as they had no paint, posters or other material. David and I were taking a well-earned break congratulating ourselves on our plans and parking arrangements when Barry Kirton sent for us.

'What time do the reliefs come from divisions gentlemen?' he asked.

'On the way Sir,' we chorused knowing that the changeover time was at the end of our break.

'Planning, Sir,' said David Blick.

'Planning? You've got every bloody van in the force parked in Steel House Lane. The reliefs have no transport!'

It was a good job the demonstrators were anarchists and by their very nature unorganised or we would have been in serious difficulty.

The adjacent location of headquarters caused me another problem. When Sir Philip Knights retired and deservedly became the first Police Life Peer, he was replaced by Geoffrey Dear, now Sir Geoffrey. We knew nothing of him other than what we had read in the newspapers and seen on television. He was a very tall, imposing figure who promised great things and we all looked forward to developments.

At 5.30pm one day, my telephone rang and I announced myself. 'Hello Mr Hannis. Geoffrey Dear.'

'Oh yes,' I said, expecting a wind-up, 'and what can I do for you?'

'I thought that I would visit your station this evening and

see some of the 2–10 shift and have a look round,' said the voice.

'It *is* him,' I thought. 'Of course Sir, what time would you like to come?'

'You can pick me up Mr Hannis, at about 8pm. I am staying at Tally Ho!'

'I'll be there Sir,' I said readily.

Don't panic! Who dare I let him see? I was blessed with my share of idiots amongst my many excellent staff. I consulted the Duty Inspector and arranged for my smartest Sergeant and a selection of Constables of varying service to be available. I checked on the night shift duty list and warned everyone in the building, kitchen, club and lock-up that the new Chief was imminent. I thought I had everything covered.

I collected the Chief and soon found that he had done his homework. He knew all about me and also that I had a second police station. I had not warned Bridge Street, thinking he would be unaware of its existence.

'I'll see 2–10 and then you can take me to Bridge Street West and we'll see the night shift out when we get back. Then you can take me out for a look at the city.'

What a programme.

It was my intention to sit in on the meeting with 2–10 in order to exercise some form of control. No chance.

'Off you go Mr Hannis,' said the Chief after my introductions. 'They won't talk freely with you here.'

'Too right,' I thought. 'That was the plan,' but off I went.

At least it gave me the chance to speak to Bridge Street West. I telephoned Bridge Street and spoke to a Sergeant. I told him what was happening and also said, 'And get the telly back in the found property.' The Sergeant protested that he did not know anything about a television, but I knew that the office man watched television in the evenings. I thought the Chief might not be too impressed.

Mr Dear was pleased with 2–10 and we drove to Bridge

Street where news of the Chief's discussions had already arrived. He had apparently encouraged the troops to tell him of their complaints and had promised action on uniforms, radios and working conditions. The old soldiers gathered at Bridge Street needed no encouragement and before long the Chief was touring the single men's quarters which he there and then decided to close! This was fine for the activists that had complained of the living conditions but I was left with the problem of re-housing a number of single officers.

We returned to Steel House Lane to see the night shift. I was able to control this much more and I stressed the constraints of time and that we could not leave the city unprotected. Mr Dear contented himself with a rousing address and promises of great change. It was nearly Henry V before Harfleur. I expected a cheer at the end.

'Nearly done,' I thought, when the Chief said, 'Shall we have a pint in the club before we go out?'

'That would be great, Sir,' I said, but thinking 'Oh no. All the drunks from the lock-up will be in there.'

The Central Lock-up was a well-known posting for the difficult and dissolute. We walked into the club. Immediate silence. The Chief beamed on everyone and said, 'What will you have Bill?'

'Mine is being pulled, Sir,' I said, noticing Ian the barman filling my glass.

The Chief had a pint and circulated. He was brilliant, he handled the drunks well and charmed everyone. It was soon time to depart and I took him on a tour of the city centre before dropping him at Tally Ho! at about midnight. A great success, but there were later repercussions due to some extravagant promises that were unachievable. This, however, came later in his reign.

Geoffrey Dear made an excellent start in the force and certainly boosted morale. I had many dealings with him over the years and he was always charming, but he could, like any successful leader, be totally ruthless.

Early in my new posting, I made a point of getting out of the office. There were a number of reasons for this: to get to know my patch on the ground; to meet officers outside the police station; to give myself some variety; and to take exercise.

The first time that I set off on foot to Bridge Street police station from the city centre, the Controller wanted to send someone with me to show me the way. The staff soon got used to me setting off, always in uniform, to roam the city centre or walk to Newtown and it gave the younger officers the chance to talk to a senior officer without a Sergeant or Inspector present. It also became my habit on a Saturday to stand at the junction of New Street and Corporation Street during the late morning and from 4.30pm until after 6pm. The city was always busy on Saturdays but especially during the football season when supporters would gather before the game giving potential for disorder. Often after a Birmingham City home game a mob of supporters, sometimes several hundred strong, would come into the city centre and attempt to seek out opposing supporters. We became adept at dealing with this but also had to monitor groups of young black men who would wait until we were occupied with football supporters and then 'steam' through stores stealing anything to hand. These challenges could be planned for but more unpredictable were the street robberies that occurred on most Saturdays.

To thwart all disorder and crime, we would parade as many as fifty officers at 11am on a Saturday, depending upon intelligence. I was duty officer on alternate Saturdays and it was then that I stood in my position at the T junction. When I first started this habit, my staff thought that I was posing and the public thought I was a bus Inspector with my flat hat and silver braid. I soon found a chance to do my 'Douglas Bader' routine.

One Saturday morning I noticed a group of five boys aged about fifteen to sixteen in deep conversation outside a shop dealing in second-hand jewellery. I saw one go into the shop and come out empty-handed from whatever his venture was. The boys took no notice of me as they walked by and I wandered after them. I saw them stop outside another jeweller's in New Street. The same boy went in and the remaining four stood in a doorway. I awaited the return of the fifth and then corralled them in the doorway. The fifth boy was holding a bag and on examination I saw that it contained some expensive-looking jewellery. They could not satisfactorily account for it and I arrested them all. I radioed for a van and a number of officers arrived, some on foot, to see this spectacle of a Superintendent with prisoners. I left the boys with other officers and went into the jeweller's and soon established that they were trying to sell the jewellery. I went with the boys in the van to Steel House Lane, booked them in with the custody Sergeant and sent for the CID. I told the CID officer to sort out the matter. The prerogative of rank! I returned to the streets. It transpired that the boys had entered the house of one boy's mother, with whom he was not living, and stolen the jewellery. A burglary by any yardstick!

The second chance to 'fly the spitfire' came a few Saturdays later. I heard on my radio that a street robbery had taken place and the offenders were being pursued by officers and heading in my direction. I immediately saw two young black men running very fast one behind the other on the other side of the road. I ran to intercept them in New Street and saw that I could not get near the first one, but I was able to reach the second one. I had him on the floor and saw a Uniform Inspector running towards me: Mick Doyle, a very quick rugby winger. 'That's the witness, boss,' he gasped as he ran by and rugby-tackled the first man. Other officers quickly joined us and despite the tension there was great hilarity that I had succeeded in catching the witness. The witness also saw the funny side of it, although I must say that my own laughter was a bit forced.

The duty rota was such that Barry Kirton was also on

duty on my duty weekends. He came in on Saturdays and took the opportunity to catch up on paperwork, but he also liked to get out whenever possible. One Saturday he arranged a rendezvous over the radio and spent some time walking about with me. He was larger than life in many ways and the sight of he and I in uniform, one eighteen to nineteen stone and the other sixteen to seventeen stone caused something of a stir and we were always noticed. There was a very busy controlled pedestrian crossing in Corporation Street outside Rackham's. On this day there were large numbers of people waiting to cross and as there was a break in the traffic, Barry stepped into the road and began to cross. I could see that everyone was going to play 'follow my leader'.

I shouted, 'The lights are red, Sir!'

Everyone but Barry stopped and he continued in solitary splendour. I crossed on green and when I reached him I could see that he was furious.

'Why did you do that? You made me look a fool,' he said.

And I said, 'There would have been an accident, everyone was following you.'

I could see that he was not happy and when we met with a uniform Constable and Sergeant, I thought he might look to turn the tables, which he did. After chatting to the officers for a minute or two, he said, 'Mr Hannis will sign your pocket-books to record our meeting. I assume they are made up?'

This was designed to show me that my officers were not up to the mark. The old practice was 'leave me a line' and a signature would be applied at the end of the shift. These two officers did not know what Barry was talking about, a Superintendent signing a pocket book in the street. I could see that they were reluctant to produce the books which were no doubt not up to date. I said, 'Leave me a line,' and Barry said, 'They could sign yours.'

'You wicked bugger,' I thought.

'I'll leave you a line as well Sarg,' I said and started to walk away.

Barry came after me. 'That was naughty,' I said.

'But funny,' said Barry.

There were always events and functions taking place at which we were required to provide a presence or full security cover, dependent upon the situation. One such event was the Annual Police Carol Service organised by the Christian Police Association. The threat level at the time was high and a full security search had been arranged. The service was to be attended by the DCC and civic dignitaries. The service was held in St Philip's Cathedral and Canon Peter Berry allowed Barry and I to occupy his pew at the back of the Cathedral. The service was going well, with nice music and singing, and then came time for an address by a 'convert', someone declaring his faith to the assembled congregation. It seemed a nice touch when a uniformed Constable ascended the pulpit steps and began to address the congregation in a strong Black Country accent.

'I was a sinner and I have been saved.' Very impressive, 'I was a lecher and a drunkard, but I have seen the light.'

Hang on a minute, this is not so good. Barry looked at me with alarm.

'I got drunk every night, I was a disgrace to my wife and family and one night when I was asleep on the floor in the kitchen, it came over me,' the Constable continued.

'I'll come over him, if I can get hold of him,' muttered Barry. 'Get him out.'

'We can't, he'll have to see it through,' I said.

The 'sermon' continued in the same embarrassing manner. We could see that the DCC was not very pleased and on his way out he said to Barry, 'Who approved that?'

'No idea, Sir, we're security,' said Barry.

It was the last Christmas Carol Service where the programme and contents were not submitted for prior approval!

There was a major demonstration one Saturday. It was

peaceful, but intense, and was South Africa-related. There was a march to take place in the afternoon and I had arranged to meet my wife and younger daughter at lunchtime to select a microwave oven, a new venture for the Hannis household. We selected the microwave from Rackham's and I arranged to collect it before closing time to transport it home. All went well with the march until in what was clearly a pre-planned action, all the marchers sat down in Steel House Lane outside the police station. It was as though we were under siege. The road was totally blocked and we had insufficient officers to remove the demonstrators. We summoned assistance and attempted to negotiate with the marchers through the windows. The cause of the sit-down was that we held a few of their number in custody due to offences of obstruction earlier in the day. The protesters demanded the release of their friends. Time was getting on and Rackham's would be closed at 6pm and no microwave. I told Barry that I had to pop out for a minute and donning a civilian jacket, picked my way through the sitting demonstrators to some cheers and ribaldry which increased greatly on my return with my microwave. Everyone was good humoured except for Barry when he realised why I had 'popped out'. He never let me forget that day and still mentions it. The demonstration ceased when we bailed the prisoners, which we would have done anyway.

To say that the job was very busy would be an under-statement. It did improve in some ways. On Pip's retirement the administrative functions were civilianised, but one area which was not an improvement, was 'Policing by Objectives'. I could see the point of setting both force and divisional objectives as this clarified the task for all ranks, but I could not see the point in changing them every year. It was confusing and time-wasting as headquarters insisted on full consultation between ranks before setting objectives. This wasted valuable policing time. Head-quarters had issued the Force Objectives, different to last year and asked for comment. There was a deadline, but I ignored it. A deputation of a Chief Inspector and an Inspector came to see me from headquarters to ask why I had not met my deadline. I told them that we were too busy policing. I knew that I could not avoid commenting on the new objectives and I wrote, 'It seems to me that there is not a lot wrong with the original objectives of Rowan and Mayne. The protection of life and property, the prevention and detection of crime and the prosecution of offenders against the peace.'

I was castigated again and this time in writing.

I had yet to complete two years in post which was normally the minimum before looking for another posting. I was not unhappy, but was becoming frustrated. The building was poor, restrictions were tight, the hours long and the challenge unremitting. I was settled to carry on when I had an unexpected telephone call from Detective Chief Superintendent Graham Trevis, the Head of Special Branch.

'Can I come over and see you?' he asked.

'Of course,' I said, knowing better than to ask a Special Branch man for information over the telephone.

When Graham arrived he said, 'Would you like to be my deputy?'

I was immediately suspicious. Why me? I did not even know that there was to be a Superintendent Deputy. I knew that the Branch had grown, but also knew that there was a DCI in the Special Branch who was highly thought of and had been a Special Branch officer in every rank. Why not him?

'Who else have you asked?' I said.

'No-one. You are my first choice,' said Graham.

'I'm flattered, but why me and why not your present deputy?' I said in response.

Graham explained that there were a number of reasons why I had been selected. There were about to be great changes in Special Branch, nationally, as Parliament had for the first time ever set 'terms of reference' for Special Branches and it was felt that I would carry them through. Graham had also been selected as security advisor to the Birmingham bid for the 1992 Olympics. This selection would require a great deal of commitment and would mean that he would be away from the force. The new Deputy would therefore be Head of Special Branch for the immediate future and because of that it was felt that the present Deputy was not the ideal choice to be promoted and given full command. I had the necessary credentials and would also not be bound by Special Branch tradition. I asked Graham who else knew of the offer and he said, 'The 7th floor,' meaning the ACPO team.

I said that I would think about it and let him know in a day or two. He kindly allowed me this time.

There were a few considerations. The main one was, 'Is it good for my career?' I consulted with my Chief Superintendent, Barry Kirton. He was firmly of the view that it was 'too early' and that I should complete at least two years at Steel House Lane. I knew that I was ready for the off and that an offer of a Detective Superintendent's job at headquarters was a good one. I was still undecided when I got a telephone call from Graham's current deputy: 'the sitting tenant'. He told me that he understood that I had been offered the post of deputy in Special Branch. I confirmed this and he went on to say, 'It's a very difficult job and with the changes that are to be made, and your lack of contact with box [MI5], I don't think you have the necessary experience to do the job without causing you problems.'

I thanked him. The cheeky bugger! A DCI telling me I couldn't do his job. That was it, the decision was made. I was in and he was out!

I rang Graham and told him of my decision, and casually asked about the sitting tenant, suggesting that it might be best if I had an unhindered passage. Graham assured me that his present deputy would be leaving for career development. Good. To be fair, I could see his position. He had been groomed for the job and I was now getting it. He knew that if I took the job, he had no chance in the future. He did very well and deservedly so, ending his career as a Detective Chief Superintendent in a southern Force where his fluency in French enabled him to provide invaluable assistance during the commissioning of the Channel Link.

Chapter Eighteen

Deputy Head of Special Branch

I took up my new position and soon saw why they needed a new broom. The terms of reference, the first ever for Special Branch, had arisen due to a number of operational problems relating to the investigation of 'innocent' parties and the keeping of files on persons who were not and never would be a threat to the security of the state. There was to be wholesale weeding of files and restrictions on future investigation and recording of organisations and persons. There was great resistance to this amongst the old guard and this led to some difficulties. There was also resentment of my appointment by some elements for like all good leaders my predecessor had his coterie of supporters. I decided that the active resistors would have to go, and over a period engineered the departure of a number of officers. I did not know, but I did develop a reputation as a 'Machiavellian character' as a result of this. No harm, for the job got done and an early test of my strategy and progress came after only six weeks in post. The HMI's office arranged an inspection by a Detective Chief Superintendent from the Metropolitan Special Branch prior to a formal inspection by the HMI and his Staff Officer. The visit was a daunting one, but I had done my homework and despite a very thorough and professional inspection by the Met man, I felt that we had come out well.

As Head of Special Branch, Graham was responsible for the Anti-terrorist Squad, the Immigration and Nationality Department, the Airport Unit and Branch Offices at Brierley Hill and Coventry. As Graham was absent these were all my responsibility and there was also an important liaison and operational function with MI5 and sometimes MI6. The Metropolitan Special Branch were responsible for Irish matters on the mainland and liaison was needed between them and the Royal Ulster Constabulary on Irish terrorism. I cannot for obvious reasons detail many of these matters, but suffice to say that it was a very interesting and far-reaching role that I had accepted.

I was told to expect a full pre-inspection visit by the HMI Staff Officer and when it came, I found that it was my old adversary from Henley and Bramshill, Jock Shaw, now Staff Officer to the HMI. I feared the worst, but he could not have been more complimentary, and he showed me a letter from the Met man which was nothing short of congratulatory. Jock told me that because of the letter, the inspection would be a formality and so it proved.

It is necessary at this stage to bring in family matters. It was not my intention, when starting these recollections, to involve my family life except in passing, but my work was so affected at that time that I must write of it.

My lovely wife had been unwell for some time, with 'women's trouble' as I glibly called it. I had arranged for her, with her agreement, to see a consultant, David Sturdee. He had arranged for her to be admitted to a private hospital for a surgical examination. This took place on a Friday and on the Saturday morning, we were told that my wife needed immediate surgery for cancer. We were both devastated. The surgery was to take place early the following week. I went into work on the Monday morning and at about 10am, Jim Burn, Detective Chief Superintendent Operations came into my office. He immediately saw that I was not my normal self and demanded to know the reason. I told him, he sent me home and I did not return for three months. I was 'working from home' with full approval from the ACPO team. During this time my wife had major surgery and radiotherapy and by the time I returned to work she was fully recovered. My wife wrote to the DCC, Les Sharpe, thanking him for my time at home. He wrote back to say, 'The job is like a bank, you put a lot in and you can always take some out.'

On my return to the office, I slipped back into my role with ease as I was fully abreast of developments through my working from home. I settled in to a very enjoyable but challenging job. The responsibilities were so varied that every day was interesting and often exciting. When Graham returned from the abortive attempt to woo the IOC to Birmingham, there was no problem in the division of responsibilities. I had control of the ATS and all ongoing SB operations. Graham dealt with policy, ACPO, MI5 and oversaw the administrative matters. We had a very good working relationship, and as he was still away from the office quite often for various demands, I took on his role in his absence.

The ATS had a number of roles, one of which was a surveillance unit for Special Branch. The Force had a dedicated surveillance unit which was extremely expert and highly rated, but they were much in demand and it was decided that the Divisional demands could not be usurped by Special Branch. The quick way to train the ATS in their new role was to recruit officers from the Force Surveillance Unit at the end of their attachment. This led to other problems, the professional surveillance officers needing not only good communications equipment, but also at least five cars and a motorcycle. The officers were using their own cars which was totally unsatisfactory. I began to come under steady daily pressure from the ATS DI and DSs to provide them with cars. Five cars cost a lot of money and the budget did not allow for such expenditure. The problem was becoming acute, as we were seriously underperforming due to lack of a full mobile surveillance capability. I began to badger the Transport Manager for cars, even redundant CID cars, anything. Eventually, the Transport Manager got fed up with me and said, 'Look, I am selling the force coach and you can have the money for cars. I expect to get somewhere around £30,000 for it.'

Wonderful. I told the ATS and they immediately began to draw up a 'wish list' of the types of cars they wanted. I took the list to the Transport Manager and told him that he should do the best he could and second-hand would be best for the ATS in order that the cars blended in with normal traffic. His eyes lit up at this and he said that he would do well for us, but we would have to accept what he provided. I did not argue as once we had a car, it would be on our inventory and would be replaced automatically at the end of its life. Five old bangers would do for me – but not for the ATS.

The cars arrived one at a time over a period of some weeks. They were fine, I thought, but the only trouble was they were all blue. The ATS said that car-switching when following a target would not be very effective with all the cars the same colour. I explained the rationale behind my strategy, but they never forgot. They presented me with a desk-top pen stand when I eventually moved on, and the stand had five blue model cars glued to it!

We became heavily involved with the Royal Canadian Mounted Police in their investigation of the loss of the Air India flight over the Atlantic off the Irish coast. The explosion on the aircraft was such that there was no trace evidence whatsoever and the investigation was incredibly difficult for the Mounties. Sikh extremists were believed responsible and we were host to a number of such groups in the West Midlands. There had been excellent co-operation between DI Jim Evans and his officers from the 'Sikh desk' and I had no involvement other than approving certain measures and being kept fully informed.

The time had arrived when a more active participation from the RCMP was required to include an officer being allocated a desk in our office. There were also provisional plans to carry out raids in relation to suspects in the West Midlands area. In order to further this, and formalise it, Jim Evans told me that an RCMP officer from the Canadian High Commission was to visit and thought it appropriate that I should meet him. I agreed and at the due time, Jim and his two officers walked into my office with the Mountie. My officers were stunned when I rose to my feet and sang, 'Oh Rose Marie I love you, I'm always dreaming of you.' They thought I had gone mad.

'Bill, that joke wore thin years ago.' It was Bob Paradis, my friend from Tally Ho! He had been promoted and returned to London for a second spell as RCMP Liaison Officer. I am sure that an old friendship cemented the liaison and in due course a major operation took place to arrest suspects and search their houses.

I commanded the operation from HQ and sadly could not visit the scenes. An RCMP Superintendent was in command of their contingent and searched a house in Coventry occupied by a Sikh employed at the Jaguar factory. When the Superintendent returned to my office, he was elated, as unbelievably the man had kept photographs in his house of explosions on Vancouver Island together with photographs of what was clearly a bomb. Not infallible evidence, but one hell of a pointer.

Special Branch were not only responsible for searches through the ATS of premises and surrounding areas prior to VIP visits, but also for the protection of the Principal in co-operation with either the Royalty Protection Group or the Metropolitan Police Special Branch. Such events were time-consuming and could be stressful, but they were also enjoyable, especially when Royalty was involved. Any criticism of the Royal Family is always countered by studying the faces of the public at these events. Sheer joy is the only description possible.

190

A very big event for us was the opening of the new Birmingham Crown Courts by HM Queen Elizabeth the Queen Mother. She was even then a great age and everyone was anxious to make the visit a success as 'it might be the last time she comes to Birmingham'. In addition to opening the new Crown Court, HM was to visit the newly refurbished Victoria Law Courts and then take lunch in the Council House.

There was a very big search and protection commitment. There was no complacency due to her Majesty's popularity. Everything had to be perfect. The Chief Constable, Geoffrey Dear, took a personal interest as he was to be present on the day and the Lord Lieutenant, Earl Aylesford, was particularly concerned that the preparations were thorough. He took the unusual step of asking to walk the route to see the problems for himself. The Chief was never one to miss a social event and invited Lord Aylesford to a buffet lunch in his office. The other lunch guests were to be Superintendent Uniform Operations, my Police Search Advisor, who was the ATS DI, myself and the Chief's Staff Officer, Mick Doyle. The Chief welcomed us and introduced us to the Lord Lieutenant, whom I knew well from my previous VIP visits. The Chief asked us what we wanted to drink. My DI and the Superintendent Ops asked for orange juice but before I could speak, the Chief said, 'Your beer's in the fridge Bill.'

I had clearly developed something of a reputation which was not unwelcome. We sat and the Chief said, 'I was just saying to Lord Aylesford, what a good year it is for sloes Bill.' I smiled.

'Do you make your own sloe gin Mr Hannis?' asked the Lord Lieutenant assuming because of the Chief's remarks that I knew something of the subject.

'I don't even brew my own beer, My Lord, never mind distil gin,' I said.

Lord Aylesford laughed, but Mr Dear was not amused.

The day of the visit was one of great excitement and

there was much jockeying between my DIs and DCIs for prime positions. I pulled rank as usual, and put my name down for lunch with the Queen Mother, along with several hundred others. I told the two DCIs that they could both attend the black tie Law Society Dinner at the Botanical Gardens on the same evening. The dinner would be an excellent terrorist target with many Judges, Barristers and other Law Officers present in large numbers. The Chief was to attend both functions.

The Queen Mother's visit went off without a hitch; large happy crowds, fine weather and altogether a wonderful day for the city. I was happy to call it a day at about 5pm and leave the evening function held to celebrate the opening of the Crown Court to the DCIs. But it was not to be.

During the afternoon, an officer on duty at the Botanical Gardens had noted a car in the vicinity. It had Irish registration and when checked showed ownership by a man in South Armagh. Whilst checks were being made with the RUC another car with Irish registration appeared in the vicinity and it was registered to the same man. The RUC told us that the man was a known Provisional IRA sympathizer. This was serious.

The Chief had by now gone home to change for dinner. I instructed that the ATS search team review the premises and remain on site. I told the DCIs, Mick Bromwich and Gordon Heatley, to carry on with their plans and I rang the Chief. I told him what had occurred and he asked if I was satisfied that the Botanical Gardens were safe. What a question!

'Yes Sir,' I said. 'Fully secure.' The die was cast.

The Chief told me to meet him at 7.15pm at the entrance to the Botanical Gardens and to have the manager of the building, the organiser of the dinner and the President of the Law Society await his arrival. I made the necessary arrangements and awaited the Chief.

I was in a lounge suit and humbly apologised for being improperly dressed on the Chief's arrival, knowing him to be a stickler for protocol.

'No matter,' he said. 'Brief me.'

I briefed him and took him to a room where the three men waited. I had told them nothing other than that the Chief wished to see them.

Geoffrey Dear was brilliant. He was offered Champagne which he accepted. I declined. I was introduced as 'My Security Specialist' and instructed to relate all measures that I had taken to protect the venue. Geoffrey then told them of the problem, and they visibly blanched especially when Mr Dear said, 'I am certain that there is no bomb in the building, but the IRA are out there and although I consider my cordon adequate, I cannot guarantee against a rocket or grenade attack against this glass building.' They were speechless as he went on, 'However, I am prepared to sit down to dinner if you are. We cannot let these people win.'

Well, there was no alternative, they had to agree. The only person leaving was me, but I did not mention that!

The organisers went about their business and Geoffrey Dear spoke with the two DCIs. He ordered that he be updated every half hour as to the state of enquiries to trace the vehicles. You can only imagine the stir caused every half hour, as a DCI rose from table to whisper in the Chief's ear.

During the evening, the cars were traced. The man in South Armagh was a car dealer and had sold the cars on their Irish plates to an Asian man in Bordesley Green. When the Chief was told, he said, 'Don't tell anyone, just keep coming up every half hour.'

I regaled my boss, Graham Trevis, with this story before he went to the Chief's morning briefing the next day. Graham had clearly told the Chief of my admiration for his style, for when I saw him later that morning, he gave me a dig in the ribs, winked and said, 'We did well last night, didn't we Bill?'

'All good for the image, Sir,' I said.

I had been Deputy Head of Special Branch for almost

two years and although I was no way unhappy, I began to think about the future. I was well regarded in the force with a reputation for being able to successfully take on difficult roles and I hoped for further promotion. There were no obvious vacancies, but I was in a front row position should anything arise that suited my talents.

I was one day at New Scotland Yard participating in a National Conference on the Arab Terrorist threat and was accompanied by my Arab specialists from the headquarters office. The conference was in full flow when I was called from the room to take a telephone call. It was the ACC (Crime) Tom Meffen.

'Bill, do you want to be a Chief Superintendent?' he said.

'Yes, Sir,' I replied without hesitation.

'Do you want to know where it is?' said the ACC.

'No Sir, I'll take it,' I answered.

There was a chuckle down the phone, 'I told the Chief you'd take it. Well done. It's a Home Office job. Come and see me tomorrow.'

I was thrilled and I rang my wife later.

Her first question was, 'Where will you be based?'

I said, 'I don't know.'

'You're hopeless,' she exclaimed. 'It could be in Timbuctoo for all you know.' But I knew she was pleased, really.

Chapter Nineteen

A National Role

It was not, as usual, as straightforward as Tom Meffen had suggested. The Chief had been asked to nominate someone for a Detective Chief Superintendent's position leading a team being formed to look at some recommendations on Scientific Support to Crime, Investigation and Detection. He had now nominated me, but I discovered that there were other candidates. There was apparently some urgency in the situation as the job was to start on leap year day, 29 February 1988, and it was now late January! I was to attend for an interview at the Home Office within a few days.

I was given a copy of the *Touche Rosse Review of Scientific Support to the Police* which had been commissioned by the Home Office and contained many recommendations. The Home Office and ACPO Crime Committee wanted a review of the recommendations to provide some further recommendations as to what to do about the first lot of recommendations. Another straightforward job! The Touche Rosse Report was in three volumes, but I soon realised that I had no chance of giving a reasoned view of its contents in time for the interview. I decided not to bother and turned up at Horseferry House in the Horseferry Road to see a Bob Cozens, the Head of the Police Requirements Support Unit (PRSU) and former Chief Constable of West Mercia, more in hope than confidence. I was interviewed by Mr Cozens and a Chief Superintendent, Mick James, from Surrey, also seconded to PRSU. It was clear after a while that nobody was too sure of what was wanted. They knew that some of the recommendations were sensible and Scientific Support was badly in need of re-organisation but they were not sure how to tackle it. Well that made three of us! I said, 'It seems to me, Sir, that you want something selling to police forces and that it needs to be practical and achievable. If that is so, then I am your man.' I got the job.

It was soon very clear that I was right and that there was no plan. I was given a substantive Superintendent who had been part of the original Touche Rosse team; he was a Manchester Officer. I was also given a temporary Detective Superintendent who was a Scene of Crime expert from West Mercia and the final member was a senior Forensic Scientist. I had no office and was offered three alternatives: a Portakabin in the yard at West Bromwich police station, an office at Shard End police station in Birmingham or a four-bedroom detached house in the drive of Hindlip Hall, the West Mercia Headquarters. No contest!

I met with the West Mercia officer, Alan Scrafton, whom I had met some years earlier when he was the Police Liaison Officer at the Birmingham Forensic Science Laboratory. Alan was a very affable, sociable, big man who was to prove a good friend, deputy and ally. The house was ideal, but we had no furniture. Mick James in London said that we could have all the furniture from the West Bromwich Portakabin as it all belonged to the Home Office. We arranged for that to be brought over and met with the other two team members for a good lunch at the Raven in Droitwich. There was clearly some team building to be done, but firstly we needed a secretary. Both Alan and the Manchester officer, Philip Machent, recommended Wendy Gwilliam who had been engaged with the Touche Rosse Review and, at that time, was a secretary at West Mercia HQ. The force were willing for her to come to us and I met with her. She was only 22 and I had some doubts, but her enthusiasm was infectious, so I took her on. I never regretted it, and she was marvellous, a true Secretary in that she could turn her hand to anything.

I sought approval to equip the office and PRSU readily agreed. I was beginning to learn that provided you were sensible, money was not a problem.

Alan had divided the office up for me, with me having a large first floor bedroom overlooking the garden, but I knew that we had to work as a team and that this was a very big task that we had been given. If it was ever to work there was no time for rank and privilege, so I put all four of us in the same room on the ground floor in what was a straight-through sitting room. We either gelled, or someone would have to go and it wouldn't be me.

I had a number of bosses: Tony Mullet, the Secretary of ACPO Crime Committee and Chief Constable of West Mercia; Bob Cozens, the Director of PRSU; and his boss Gordon Wasserman, an Assistant Under Secretary of State at the Home Office. My report was to be submitted and presented to a ACPO Crime Committee for approval and then hopefully implementation of my recommendations. Another easy job!

There were two immediate tasks – firstly to dissect the Touche Rosse Report and to decide how to tackle the overall problem, and secondly to assess the current situation in the United Kingdom first hand.

I decided to split the recommendations of the original report and write a new report on each and present them separately. I felt that this would ensure that they would be read and that also it would mean that I had provided an early result. As part of my original plan, I proposed visiting nineteen police forces in England and Wales to examine their scientific support structure and discuss with every command level the way ahead. It was also planned to visit all seven Forensic Science Laboratories during the same phase.

The plan was approved and we set off, the three policeman and one scientist. It was a great success from a team-building viewpoint and an eye-opener in that there was no standardisation of practice, training or strategy whatsoever.

The team decided to take the best force in each discipline; Scenes of Crime, Fingerprints and Photography, as an example of 'best practice', and build on these as the model for our recommendations.

There was great support for our endeavours in every area, except Fingerprints. Fingerprints had always been a mystery to me in that I knew of the need for 16 points of coincidence sequence between the scene mark and the file fingerprint before an identification could be proved in court, but I had no idea of how the Fingerprint Bureaux were run. We soon found that it was a shambles. The statistics were massaged and in the main the Bureaux were unproductive and protective of the mystique of fingerprint identification.

An example of one murder investigation well illustrates the antiquity and intransigence of thinking of the senior fingerprint experts.

A prostitute had been murdered in a large provincial city. The murder had taken place in a flat where clear finger marks had been found on wallpaper by use of a then new method of fingerprint visualisation. The marks were certain to be those of the offender. The Senior Investigating Officer demanded that the Fingerprint Bureau tell him whether the offender had previous convictions and could therefore be identified. The bureau in question took a whole year to search the paper data base and did no other work whatsoever during this time. This meant that no other marks from scenes of crime in the whole force area was searched for a year! There was no sub-division of the paper files by either age or sex which resulted in the fingerprints of women and old men being searched against marks from a murder and rape of a woman. This was symptomatic of almost the whole of the fingerprint service with a few notable exceptions.

I discovered that fingerprints in the United Kingdom were controlled by the National Conference of Fingerprint Experts through their committee, a group of die-hard long-serving men who met regularly at New Scotland Yard under the Chairmanship of a civilian fingerprint officer in a position with equivalent status to a Commander in the Metropolitan Police. I sought permission to attend their meetings from ACPO Crime Committee which was readily given. Alan Scrafton and I began to attend. We were not welcome and patronised that we would not understand the technicalities of their discussions. I resented this attitude.

It became apparent that the meetings were an excuse for a social gathering and drinks before a hearty lunch in the Senior Officers mess at New Scotland Yard. The committee clearly believed that my work would have no effect on their supremacy in fingerprint matters. They controlled training and standards, they also held the National Register of Fingerprint Experts. I believed that they were obstructive to my work in trying to take the whole of scientific support forward as a unit and their work was to remain as a superior elite.

The crunch came at a meeting where they were to discuss the 'Hinder Report', a damning review of Fingerprint Bureaux citing total inefficiency and complacency. The report had been commissioned by the National Audit office with whom Alan and I had discussed it.

The day of the important meeting arrived. The Hinder Report was an item low down on the morning's Agenda and I awaited the discussion with interest. I was amazed: the discussion took less than ten minutes and mainly consisted of a series of derogatory remarks about the author and his abilities. I said, 'Is this it? The most important report ever written on fingerprints and you have dismissed it in less than ten minutes.'

I was patronised for lack of understanding the problem. I had had enough of these dinosaurs and said, 'You are a disgrace. I'll get rid of you lot.' I was fuming. They laughed and ridiculed my threats. Wrong thing to do!

Some months later, I presented a paper to the ACPO Crime Committee. I was by this time well regarded by the committee and my short reports were welcomed as clear and simple. The current paper was mainly concerned with the establishment of Scientific Support Units with civilian scientists as managers. It would be a combined unit of Scenes of Crime (SOCO), Photography and Fingerprints. The report was unanimously approved. I had put in a recommendation that 'the National Conference of Finger-print Experts be disbanded and replaced by a National Conference of Scientific Support'. It was a logical and sensible move which I neglected to mention in my presentation. The whole report had been approved and I asked an eminent Chief Constable, 'When will you tell the fingerprint people about their conference, Sir?' He was nonplussed and I pointed out the relevant paragraph to him. 'You crafty bugger,' said the CC, 'I'll do it. Their conference is coming up soon.' I knew that of course.

I could not conceal my satisfaction when in his address to the conference at Lewes he announced the new arrangements. I did not help by calling their final dinner 'The last supper'.

This was not to be the end of my battle with some senior fingerprint experts, but it was the first of a number of victories.

We had only been in business for a couple of months when I received a telephone call from Chief Superintendent Mick James at PRSU asking whether I would like to go to Paris. I readily accepted before asking the purpose of the visit. There was to be an Interpol conference at their head-quarters in St Cloud, Paris on identification methods. The Home Office rightly thought that as the main purpose of scientific support was to identify offenders, we should attend.

Alan Scrafton and I were booked into a hotel in Paris and flew out from Birmingham where we posed for a photograph on the tarmac next to a Harrier Jump Jet before setting off. We flew on a Sunday in order to be ready for the opening of the conference on the Monday morning. I was in a state of high excitement for you will remember that I was not widely travelled. I was not only excited by visiting Paris for the first time, but by being a delegate to an Interpol Conference. Interpol was always portrayed as a shadowy International Force of Supercops, but was in reality an administrative organisation. This knowledge did not however dampen my enthusiasm.

The late booking of our places meant that Alan and I did not have a programme or list of delegates and it was not until our accreditation at St Cloud on Monday morning that I saw the wide range of subject matter and world-wide distribution of delegates. The majority of European countries were represented as were North America, North and South Africa and China.

There was a welcome from the long-serving director of Interpol, Ray Kendal, and the Chairman of the Conference, a Chief Superintendent from Canada, began to deal with administrative matters. It was then that I began to wonder at the quality of the programme.

'Put your hands up if you are stopping for lunch,' was the first item. Stopping for lunch? Did they think we were going home? It was hardly a local seminar.

'One or two of the speakers have been unable to attend and if anyone would like to fill in, they would be welcome,' said the chairman.

Fill in, what on? These were extremely specialised areas and hardly suitable for an off-the-cuff chat.

To be fair, much of the input was of high quality and very interesting, but the fill-in from Canada on 'the identification of skidoo tracks' was somewhat lost on those from temperate and tropical climes as was 'the identification of glove marks'. As a Zimbabwian officer put it, 'They don't wear gloves much down our way.'

But the first prize had to go to the Chinese presentation

on facial reconstruction, a technique then in its infancy. The presentation was eagerly awaited, but sadly Chinese is not an official Interpol language and the Chinese did not speak any of the four official languages. It was highly embarrassing for all concerned.

The highlights made up for the disasters and the weather was wonderful. Alan and I met some very useful contacts for the future especially in the field of fingerprints. I was to return to Paris several times before my retirement and each visit was a great pleasure and a learning experience.

There was no doubt that I had a great job and all I had to do was produce the goods. We produced reports at regular intervals, all of which were accepted, and there began to be implementation throughout England and Wales. The only area of conflict continued to be fingerprints. I had been instructed at an early stage to attach myself to a review of the 16-point standard of fingerprint evidence being carried out by Ray Williams, a retired Director of the Metropolitan Science Laboratory who was being assisted by Ian Evett, a statistician from the Forensic Science Laboratory at Aldermaston. The teaching in fingerprint training was that the likelihood of two fingerprints of different persons being the same was sixteen to the power of sixteen against, a number which was said to be more than twice the population of the world. This made fingerprint evidence infallible. The two scientists were assisted by a senior fingerprint expert from New Scotland Yard.

There was great resistance to the 'unnecessary' review from the fingerprint world in the UK. It was necessary, however, because there was a practice of 'phoning out' identifications where there were 8 points in coincidence sequence, but the expert would not back this up in court. 'Phoning out' was a method whereby the Fingerprint Bureau would telephone the officer on the case and identify the offender, but decline to back this up in writing. The question was, 'Why, if the expert was certain at 8, would he not go to court with less than 16?'

I was being 'blinded by science' in my meetings with experts and decided that I needed one of my own who could be objective and give me a clear view. I persuaded West Midlands to second a Senior Expert, Ray Broadstock, to my team for the duration. He was invaluable in clarifying matters for us and we began to make progress.

Ray Williams had discovered by examination of files at New Scotland Yard that the original standard for fingerprint identification was 12, but that in May 1923 the standard had been changed to 16 after a copy of two fingerprints from different persons in a book by Bertillon, the originator of identification by the measurement of long bones, purported to show 14 points in coincidence sequence. These photographs had been sent to NSY by an officer in New Zealand.

The then head of fingerprints at NSY had written to the commissioner, 'The standard should be raised to 16 to prevent our provincial colleagues making a wrong identification.'

NSY never told New Zealand and they still work to a standard of 12.

A review found different standards throughout Europe, with two standards in France. The USA, Canada, South Africa and Israel were different again. When you realise that the use of fingerprints in crime detection originated in India and was brought to the Metropolitan Police from there, how can there be so many variations?

Ian Evett regularly asked, 'What is a point?' There was no definitive answer. How then, he asked, could there be a standard if no-one knew what a point was? He devised a test to be taken by all fingerprint experts in the United Kingdom with more than ten years' experience. The test was also to be sent to France, Holland, Germany, Israel, the USA and Canada.

The test was simple. Ian obtained 9 marks from scenes of crime and nine fingerprints of offenders, all of whom had been convicted. He also fabricated a mark and a match.

The test was sent out with a guarantee of anonymity with two simple questions for each of the ten pairs of marks.

1. Is it an identification?
2. If yes, how many points in coincidence sequence?

The results were frightening. No-one, thank God, was fooled by the spurious mark, but the variation on the other nine was incredible. There was clearly no standard at all. What to do with the results?

Whilst the test was taking place, Ray Williams had been trying to find an edition of the Bertillon book to examine the 2 marks that caused the introduction of the 16-point standard. Professor Pierre Margot from Lausanne had found a copy of the book. He was so excited that he rang Ian Evett to tell him that the Bertillon marks were forgeries and that the points of sequence had been drawn in with a pen!

We were now in a position where we had a standard based on a forgery and total inconsistency in the application of the so-called standard. It was now clear why there was a reluctance to reduce from 16 points to 8. One thing we were certain of was that the present system could not convict an innocent man, but it was certainly failing to identify and convict many, many offenders.

The next step was to present the findings to a full meeting of the ACPO Crime committee. This took place at Cambridge and as I was not part of the original review, I was not a signatory to the report. The presentation was made by Ray Williams and Ian Evett. It was a riveting report and at the end, there was a stunned silence followed by many questions. After some time, David Owen, the chairman of Crime Committee and Chief Constable of North Wales, called me on to the podium and said, 'Bill, tell us what we have got to do. We cannot publish this.'

I gave my view of the whole subject of fingerprints, the training, certification of experts and testing of experts, all of which Ian Evett, Alan Scrafton and I had discussed at length. It was agreed that the 'show' must go on the road, i.e. that Ian Evett and I would take the 16-point review and present it at a number of regional locations in order that every Fingerprint Expert in the country would hear the review at first hand. This would ensure that there would be no misinformation and that recommendations as to training, standards, testing and other implications could be fully discussed and that in the interim, the report on the 16-point standard would not be published.

At the conclusion of the presentations which included visits to Wiesbaden, Paris and The Hague, an update was given to the ACPO Crime Committee together with a report on the suggested future for fingerprint training, which was approved. The result was that all fingerprint expert training was removed from the Metropolitan Police District as was the National Register of Fingerprint Experts. The removal was to Durham where a National Scientific Support Training Centre staffed by scenes of crime experts and forensic scientists had been established. It was further agreed that the 16-point review would not be published until all the new training and verification procedures had been well established. I am not sure how the report was eventually released, but the first I knew of it was seeing Ben Gunn, the Chief Constable of Cambridgeshire, being interviewed on television about it. He was able to say that the circumstances which had caused the problems revealed by the authors had been fully rectified. The sting was fully removed and few ripples were caused in the Scientific Support pond.

All of our work surrounding fingerprints had emphasised a desperate need for technology to aid the searching of the large Force and National databases which were almost all paper-based. There were some very limited technical aids but a new approach was needed. It was obvious that a national system for the United Kingdom was the way forward, but with some forty-five independent bureaux and no worth-while national system, the task was enormous.

The Home Office decided to research a National Automatic Fingerprint Recognition system (AFR). The computer-based system would need a detailed user requirement before the technical solution could be attempted. The Scientific Support Team was considered to be a success and I was asked to take charge of the task to write a user requirement. The Assistant Under Secretary of State, Gordon Wasserman, was well aware of my technological limitations and instructed his scientific staff to provide me with some consultants. I arrived at the Home Office one day to meet them. I was once again amazed: there was a room full of people, experts from three different companies, several from each and all on large daily fees. We had a brain-storming session and it was agreed that we had to find out what the customer wanted. It was a user requirement, the user was the police; we needed a National Conference.

It was clear at this stage that money was not a problem and a workshop weekend was arranged. A large Midlands hotel was booked and every police force in the UK sent an ACPO rep, a Senior Detective and a Senior Fingerprint Expert. My consultants and my staff acted as facilitators and the delegates provided the 'rapporteurs'. I was pleasantly surprised – my initial reaction that 'a committee could not decide anything' was wrong. There were some excellent ideas and I came away feeling that I knew the basic structure of the user requirement. I dread to think what it cost, but it was certainly a success.

A consultants' report was produced, but I knew what I wanted to do. I intended to write a basic document and 'hawk it' around the country, having small workshops and ending with another big workshop of mainly fingerprint experts. What I did not need was an army of consultants. One young man from PA, Nick Thornton, had impressed me greatly. I asked for him to be attached to us and the rest be paid off. This was agreed with the proviso that Nick's line manager at PA would have to be involved. I agreed providing that I was in charge.

The project was a great success. Nick was the technocrat and I the pragmatist. My staff were excellent as usual and after much talking and travelling, including France and Holland, a National User Requirement was produced and accepted. This turned out to be the easy part: implementation was going to be an enormous and in my time, insurmountable problem.

It is necessary once again to bring my private life into these recollections. My wife became ill again in October 1989. We had been confident that she was in full remission, but as is often the case an emotional shock seemed to trigger the disease. Doreen's father had died on her birthday. She was very distressed and I remain convinced that this was the trigger.

Surgery was necessary and I was informed that she had only six weeks to live. My lovely mother-in-law and I decided to keep my wife at home and once again the job allowed me to work from home. I will always be grateful to Lionel Grundy and Gordon Wasserman for this. My wife survived for over five months before succumbing to the dread disease, and after a period of leave with my daughters I returned to work.

This Scientific Support Team had been extremely rewarding and every one of our recommendations were accepted and implemented. We had far-reaching effects on the whole of scientific support both within and without police forces which are still felt today. Tony Mullet, Chief Constable of West Mercia and later chairman of ACPO Crime, was kind enough to say before his retirement that, 'Your team was the best thing ACPO ever did in my time.'

There were a number of ongoing tasks from our original work which I called 'the too hard to do pile'. They related to standardised terms and conditions for employers which was an impossible task across forty-three police forces. We had managed to get ourselves involved in a number of ancillary issues over the years: interview training, audio and video recording of interviews, detective training and the writing of new syllabi for fingerprint and scenes of crime training, but despite all these tasks I was getting itchy feet. It was now late spring of 1991 and sure enough just like Mr Micawber, 'something turned up'.

Tony Mullett, now the former Chief Constable of West Mercia, had retired to become the first director of the National Criminal Intelligence Service (NCIS). His first task was to head the development team and construct the service from the floor up: objectives, job description, staffing, locations, buildings and equipment. The intention was to bring together all intelligence matters including Customs and Excise under one umbrella. Tony telephoned me out of the blue.

'Bill, I am looking for a Chief Superintendent to lead the development team for NCIS. Will you apply?'

I asked why, as I knew that the post had been advertised and there had been a good response. Tony told me that there was no outstanding candidate and that it was being re-advertised. I told him I had not applied previously as the post was in London and my circumstances with a fourteen-year-old daughter at home precluded me from living in London. Tony assured me that if successful he was sure that something suitable could be arranged.

I agreed to apply and Tony told me that I was certain to be interviewed. He also said that he would be on the panel but would not ask me any questions because of our previous association. I must point out that he was not 'Tony', but 'Sir' at the time and our association was Detective Chief Superintendent to Secretary and then Chairman of ACPO Crime Committee. Hardly close friends!

I wrote my application, knowing little of the task. I stressed my long time interest in intelligence, shades of Wolfson! I mentioned my appointment of Crime Intelligence Officer at Nuneaton, Crime Squad, Special Branch and Drug Squad experiences, all intelligence-related roles.

I was called for interview at the Home Office in Queen

Anne's Gate and as I walked into an ante room a Detective Chief Superintendent from a southern Force said to me, 'Are you here for NCIS?' I confirmed that I was and he said, 'I've wasted my time, I've just been in. Had I known you were coming, I wouldn't have bothered.'

He left. I was surprised, but quite pleased; I knew that I had acquired quite a high profile but did not know I was that good!

The panel was Tony Mullet, a Senior Civil Servant and Neil Dickens, the National Co-Ordinator Regional Crime Squads. Mr Dickens opened the batting with, 'I have your application here Mr Hannis and I see that you were a crime intelligence officer in the 60s. You must have invented it.'

I knew then that I was in. There were many questions, but the majority were of a type allowing me to 'blow my own trumpet'. I left feeling very confident.

I was offered the post a week or so later and accepted. I soon learned that this was to be no 'Bobby's Job' either. I was to be the operational head of the team developing the NCIS project. Tony Mullet was to be much engaged in politics although he directed everything I did.

Politics was clearly a major factor in my selection, I heard following my appointment. There were a number of factions in the construction of NCIS. The two major ones were the Metropolitan Police and the Customs and Excise. The Met learned that they were to relinquish their control by command and co-location at NSY of a number of intelligence functions, such as the NDIIU, formerly the CDIIIU, technical operations, Football Intelligence, Crime Intelligence, Interpol and Number 9 RCS. Potential resistance would come from relocation plans and sharing information particularly with the Customs and Excise and in addition a provisional officer was to be the director of NCIS. The latter was alleviated to a great extent by the appointment of Simon Crawshaw as the Deputy Director – a very able, effective and highly regarded Metropolitan Detective. I soon learned that it was intended that much of the remainder were to be alleviated by my 'persuasive powers' demonstrated during my time on the scientific support team.

The Customs and Excise were to have a senior member of their Investigation Division on the development team at my level, although I was to be officer in charge of the working team. The man appointed was unknown to me but he was fully aware of my background and in particular my good relationships with his colleagues during my time on the Drug Squad.

The team was based in Pimlico. There were a wide range of officers from provincial Forces, the Met and Customs and Excise. Remarkably we soon gelled, tasks were allotted and work began. It was a huge task and the greatest resistance was from those who saw NCIS as a National Police Force. It took much time and effort to convince people that NCIS was an intelligence organisation with no operational function. The task was to gather, assess and disseminate crime intelligence. Others acted upon it.

I was thoroughly enjoying my role and felt that we were being very effective. There are many documents available on the structure and operations of NCIS and I do not intend to repeat them here. Suffice to say that it has and is achieving the objectives originally set.

The drawback for me was that I lived in Solihull and the office was in Pimlico. I commuted on the days I was working in London which were the majority. There was a great deal of travel throughout the UK, but my base was London. My normal day was to leave home at 6.45am and never return before 8.30pm, Monday to Friday. This was hard work but no problem to me, but I had a fourteen-year-old daughter at home. Our weekends were full and she made no complaint. However, after about four months, my elder daughter telephoned and told me that she felt that my continued absence was having an effect on my younger daughter. I knew that there must be a serious potential problem, otherwise my elder daughter would not have telephoned, she being away from home in Manchester.

I spoke at length with my younger daughter that same evening and the next morning I went in to see Tony Mullet and asked to be released. I told him my reasons and he reluctantly agreed. There was however, no job for me in the West Midlands. I was supernumerary. Tony Mullet rang my Chief, now Ron Hadfield, later Sir Ronald, and told him of my dilemma. The Chief said, without hesitation, 'Tell him to come and see me on Monday morning, I'll find him a job.'

I was very relieved and left my post within two days.

My return to force was in December 1991. I had left in February 1988; I was well past Jack King's 'three years and it's who?' and had no idea what to expect from the Chief. I was a substantive Detective Chief Superintendent, but over establishment. I knew that there were no vacancies at my rank in either CID or Uniform and I had no wish to be a 'spare dinner'. I had no wish to embarrass Ron Hadfield. My only concern was for my daughter and I had said through Tony Mullett that I would retire on my 49th birthday, 3 April 1992, and would not therefore interfere with Mr Hadfield's long-term plans.

I had an early appointment with the Chief and found him very kind and welcoming. He made it clear that I would be of great use to him 'looking after the AFR thing'. There had been considerable progress on AFR since I had written the user requirement. The Home Office had yet to authorise an official system and a group of Chief Constables, as a result of my incessant lobbying that fingerprints were not value for money had decided to obtain a system using a consortium approach. John Hoddinott, the Chief Constable of Hampshire, was the prime mover in this consortium and they were in a procurement process.

Mr Hadfield explained that he wanted me to look after the force interests in their role as a member of the consortium. I was to report to ACC Frank Wilkinson who sat on the ACPO working group of the consortium. He further explained that I had been allocated a desk in the office of the scientific support manager, Dr Chris Fouweather. Then almost as an aside, he said, 'You can give John Hoddinott a hand as well, he wants you to help him.'

Politics had been at work very quickly. I had only been available for three days and I was already back in a national role.

The job was to be very demanding, again! I found that I was to be virtually in charge of the practical side of the project with others including my old friend Nick Thornton having responsibility for the technical side.

The overall task was to obtain and assess tenders for the consortium AFR solution from companies and reduce this to a short list from which a full assessment of the final bids would be made before selection by the consortium members of a successful bidder, following a presentation meeting at the Staff College, Bramshill.

There was once again a lot of travelling involved and I began to wonder if I had made the right decision in leaving NCIS.

My task in simple terms as the process progressed, was to 'see if it worked'. That is, did the kit on offer identify offenders from marks at scenes of crime? This required the assessment of working systems at sites nominated by the bidders and in the final short list, these were in North America. I visited sites in France, Finland and Holland before an extended trip to visit working sites in Los Angeles, San Francisco, Ottawa and New York. A very enjoyable experience. I was accompanied by Detective Superintendent Graham Smith and CI Ray Elvey, two competent and likeable companions.

The process became quite feverish as there were personalities within the group who were potentially disruptive, but my rank enabled me to avoid any clashes, although matters became somewhat fraught from time to time.

The timetable was such that the Bramshill presentations by the three final short list companies were to take place on my last working weekend in the police service. The team had a sweep on how many forces represented at the weekend would sign up to the contract with the selected company. Ever the optimist, I put my money on a one hundred per cent yes vote.

The presentations were made and the findings of the tendering process assessments were reported. These had been very strict and, for example, required me to send my assessment marks under the various criteria back to Hampshire on the day of completing each site visit.

The presentations were of a very high standard as one would expect from multinational companies. These were then followed by various technical members of our working group and several Chief Officers. There was clearly no consensus on which company was pre-eminent. There was a large gathering with several representatives from each of some thirty-eight forces.

I did not have a speaking slot, but was pleased when a Chief Constable asked from the floor, 'What does Bill think?'

I knew well that certain elements did not want 'Bill' to be allowed to say what he thought. Too late – I was on!

I adopted my normal stance. I had once been described by John Over, the Chief Constable of Gwent, as, 'My Chinese friend, Ah But. We listen to all the talk and complications and then Bill says, ah but what about. . .'

I said to the meeting, 'There is only one question. Does it work?'

There were many nods of agreement.

'The simple answer is one doesn't, one does but very slowly and one does.'

I then went on to explain what I had found on my visits, emphasising that the test was scenes of crime marks, partial fingerprints. All the systems could quickly and accurately identify full sets of fingerprints from persons or bodies. What was needed was to identify offenders and only one did that at anything like the standard required. I pointed out that no-one in the world had tested the system with the volume of work that we would be using, but one system, Morpho, did work.

The meeting voted unanimously to accept the IBM/Morpho bid and everyone signed up. I won the money!

Sadly, I must mention, although it does not fit chronologically, that the IBM/Morpho system was never allowed to work properly. The whole project became a mess, bogged down in argument over contractual detail and performance levels. The needs of the police were overridden by administrative and financial demands. The IBM/Morpho Senior management were unbelievably weak in the face of pressure from a comparatively junior police officer and the demands of the users were completely ignored. The men who used the system daily knew what was required to make it work, but they were shouted down.

Back to brighter things, this was now my last week as a policeman a lovely week in many ways, but sad also. Much drink was taken at various locations.

The most poignant moment for me came on Friday 3 April 1992, my 49th birthday. By sheer coincidence, my last task was to participate in a meeting between IBM/Morpho and the consortium working group at Leek Wootton, the Headquarters of the Warwickshire Constabulary.

When I rose to speak, I began by telling the meeting that it was thirty years to the day since I had been sworn in as a member of the Warwickshire Constabulary on my 19th birthday and here I was in the same place today. When I had finished, the Warwickshire Detective Chief Superintendent, Colin Port, rose and spoke. He said that he had not known of the coincidence, but on hearing me speak he had sent out for a Warwickshire Constabulary plaque which he presented to me. I have it on my wall alongside one from the West Midlands presented to me by Ron Hadfield when I had taken leave of him earlier in the week.

For some administrative reason, we were at that time required to retire on a Sunday. My certificate of service records thirty years and two days!

Lightning Source UK Ltd.
Milton Keynes UK

177758UK00001B/10/A